JESUS
Really is Coming Back.....
SOON!

Doyle W Flowers Jr.
Operation GoTo Press
Atlanta, GA

Jesus Really Is Coming Back.....Soon!

ISBN # 978-1-60743-764-2
Copyright © 2009 Doyle W Flowers Jr.

V2.0

All Scriptures are taken from the Holy Bible,
New King James Version (recommended by God!)

Cover Design
Denise Glass
Susan Lobachyov

Interior Formatting
Toth Agency, Inc.

Publisher
Operation GoTo Press
Atlanta, GA

Library of Congress Control Number: 2009902677

Printed in the United States of America

This book may not be reproduced, transmitted, or stored in whole or in part by any means, including graphic, electronic, or mechanical without the express written consent of the publisher except in the case of brief quotations embodied in critical articles and reviews

DEDICATION

I dedicate this book to the Ancient of Days, our loving Creator. Even when one tries to use all of the beautiful words of the English language, the treasure that has been given us through Jesus Christ is quite literally unspeakable. The Bible tells us in 2nd Corinthians 9:15, "Thanks be to God for His indescribable gift". Truly to God be the Glory!

> I have a special needs request to ask of the many Prayer Warriors I know who are out there. This is a request not revealed here but is known to God. I ask that you send your prayers up the Great Throne Room of the Almighty on my behalf. The Lord has assured me that it will be answered but only by prayer. You will be rewarded if you pray in your closet (see Matthew 6:6) and I will be granted my desire. Bless you!

www.jesusreallyiscomingbacksoon.com
For additional paperbacks/hardbacks
call 24 hours 1-800-632-8437

FOR SPEAKING ENGAGEMENTS
both USA and internationally you can write:
Doyle W Flowers Jr.
P.O. Box 675071, Marietta GA 30006 or call 770-984-1565

PREFACE

There is so much I wish to share with you all in this book. I am including both personal experiences and Truths that the Almighty has taught me. William Tyndale desired that the one who pushed the plow knew the Scriptures. Although the issues dealt with here are very deep, I will attempt to make them clear to the layman and theologian alike. I will try to keep these Great Truths basic in this edition and perhaps expand them in a later book. I will reveal Truths that God has shown me directly and will offer speculation on other issues. I will also try to make clear the difference between what I am sure of and my speculation (though I believe it is correct). It is my hope and prayer that all who read this book will give their most serious consideration to these Truths. Truly to God be the Glory!

CONTENTS

1. Early Signs of His Return 1
2. God's Call. 4
3. The Blessed Hope 18
4. Time of Return 39
5. Chronological Order of Events. 56
6. Your Most Important Decision Ever . . . 98
7. To God Be The Glory! 108

Chapter One
Early Signs of His Return

I suppose that I first began looking around and noticing events briefly in the late 70s when I was in my early 20s. I remember one thing that specifically intrigued me was the advent of that special tool of communication, the television. Although this was before it was such a common belief as far as I knew, I began wondering if perhaps God was about to return. I knew little of the details of the Bible at that time. It is all about God's timing, more on that later.

Sometime after this, the knowledge of the rebirth of the nation of Israel became known to me. Though I did not become aware of the significance of that fact prophetically until later. As the years went on and the more I read and studied prophecy books, the more fascinated I became with the subject. I can remember being hardly able to wait to get home and absorb more. Keeping up with numerous authors, I looked forward to their next book of prophecy to come out with such great fervor. The more I looked and studied the more I saw that pointed to His return soon. As time went on this belief spread through our ranks and prophecy no doubt became more popular. Though many of us have suspected His return was close, no one seemed to have a complete handle on it. As I reflect on this period in my life it seems that God has been preparing us for His second coming in a subtle way. And He seems to have done this in the Holy Scriptures as well, as no one else could. Proverbs 25:2 tells us "It is the Glory of God to conceal a matter, but the glory of Kings is to search out a matter".

The Holy Scriptures are often a complicated set of writings that can and will only be understood correctly spiritually and chronologically with the Spirit of God's help. In John 14:26 we are told "But the Helper, the Holy Spirit, whom the Father will send in My name He will teach you all things, and bring to your remembrance all things that I said to you". The Lord, as He often does, admonishes us in 2nd Timothy 2:15 "Be diligent to show yourselves approved to God, a worker who does not need to be ashamed, rightly dividing the Word of Truth". Also in Hebrews 11:6 we find out "But without faith, it is impossible to please Him, for he who comes to God must believe that He is, and that He is a rewarder of those who diligently seek Him".

I have observed over the years through readings the Almighty led me to that a true understanding of the Scriptures has increased significantly over the last 100 years or so. Many have spent their lifetimes studying the Bible without understanding all the wealth of the Bible, the Book of all books. God has obviously withheld some comprehension of the Scriptures for His Purpose. I have a deep love for God and His writings, and with Him having given us all the Canon of the Holy Scriptures, I have no doubt He will give us full understanding when the time is right. Though I am not sure when, I believe this will be in the not-to-distant future, probably at a time very close to His return. He did tell me He was in a hurry, however I think God's hurrying and our hurrying are quite different! Truly to God be the Glory!

Chapter 2
GOD's call

I was called into the body of Christ at a fairly young age. A lovely young lady, who made herself available to God, with some persistence, led me to Christ. It was a difficult time in my life having moved away from home at a tender age. Going through this tumultuous time made a lasting impression in my life, particularly with me being born-again! As this lovely prodded me (led by God), I knelt down and asked Jesus to come into my heart believing in Him. It was not until later that I realized God saved my soul that very moment. That night and for the following two or so, I had the most peaceful sleep ever. What a major difference I experienced in my life! I have never forgotten those first few sweet nights even though I, as many do, backslid back into the world's ways. This caused me later to doubt my conversion as I puzzled over why I would do this. It was when I learned according to Ephesians 4:22-24, "that you put off, concerning your formal conduct, the old man which grows corrupt according to the deceitful lusts, and be renewed in the spirit of your mind, and that you put on the new man which was created according to God, in true righteousness and holiness".

For those who claim to be saved, I encourage you to do as we are admonished in 2nd Corinthians 13:5-6, "Examine yourselves as to whether you are in the faith. Test yourselves. Do you not know yourselves, that Jesus Christ is in you(?) ...unless indeed you are disqualified. But I trust that you will know that we are not disqualified".

I have learned not only from Scripture, but my own Christian walk that God has a lot of patience. I went through quite a number of times backsliding and was more than what I would put up with. Although I did not realize it at the time, I can now look back and see the chastening Hand of God in my life. God knew my heart and that I was serious about wanting to do right, as He was working in me, but I just kept falling into periods of sinful behavior. Jesus tells us in Matthew 26:41, "Watch and pray, lest you enter into temptation. The Spirit indeed is willing, but the flesh is weak." God inspired Paul to tell us in Romans 7:15-25, "For what I am doing, I do not understand. For what I will to do, that I do not practice; but what I hate, that I do. If, then, I do what I will not to do, I agree with the law that it is good. But now, it is no longer I who do it, but sin that dwells in me. For I know that in me (that is, in my flesh) nothing good dwells; for to will is present with me, but how to perform what is good I do not find. For the good that I will to do, I do not do; but the evil I will not to do, that I practice. Now if I do what I will not to do, it is no longer I who do it, but sin that dwells in me. I find then a law, that evil is present with me, the one who wills to do good. For I delight in the law of God according to the inward man. But I see another law in my members, warring against the law of my mind, and bringing me into captivity to the law of sin which is in my members. O wretched man that I am! Who will deliver me from this body of death? I thank God .... through Jesus Christ our Lord! So then, with the mind I myself serve the law of God, but with the flesh the law of sin."

In the past I used these verses more than once as an excuse to sin and I would like to impress upon you that this is not at all recommended! I can say without a doubt that I would not have put up with my behavior. The Bible tells us that there is none like Him! Isaiah 46:9 states, "Remember the former things of old, for I am God, and there is no other; I am God, and there is none like Me."

I feel certain that because God knew later what would happen, He saved me from death in an automobile accident when I was in my teens. The State Patrol that stopped to investigate marveled that we were not badly hurt. We had attended an Evangelical meeting during our trip (not planned) and I was given a little red booklet containing the plan of salvation. When the vehicle stopped after the accident, I can remember that the booklet was resting on me. I thought about that many times afterwards along with the mercy of God. Isaiah 46:10 tells us God is "Declaring the end from the beginning; and from ancient times things that are not yet done, saying, 'My counsel shall stand, and I will do all My pleasure'."

Now let me take you to a most interesting time in my life. It was perhaps 15 years ago that something very significant happened in my life. It was just a few years ago that I fully realized what this meant. I had a vivid dream one night. There were three identical tornados. Just before I woke up, I was taken up by the middle one. Although at this time God did not confirm it (as He did later), I understood the tornados to represent the triune God, God the Father, God the Son, and God the Holy Spirit. With me being taken up by the middle tornado, I knew that this represented the Lord Jesus and that the rapture would occur in my lifetime. Our being gathered to the Lord Jesus in the air is commonly called the rapture even though that specific word is not found in the Bible. The English word rapture comes from a Latin word meaning 'caught up'. Some wonderful passages are contained in 1st Thessalonians 4:16-18, "For the Lord Himself will descend from heaven with a shout, with the voice of an archangel, and with the trumpet of God. And the dead in Christ will rise first. Then we who are alive and remain shall be caught up together with them in the clouds to meet the Lord in the air. And thus we shall always be with the Lord. Therefore comfort one another with these words." The Lord later confirmed (about two years ago) that the rapture would indeed happen while I was alive and the fact that He called me as a prophet. More on this later.

More than once I pondered why God did not seem to speak out publicly as He had in the Old and New Testaments. I remember a movement years ago asking if God was dead or declaring He was. I have Good News, He was but He isn't now! Jesus has told us in Revelation 1:18, "I am He who lives, and was dead, and behold I am alive forevermore. Amen. And I have the keys of Hades and of Death." It seems that just when I came to the conclusion that God had spoken to us, through the Bible, it began.

In my earlier years I was instructed by my Mother to speak to my Grandmother about Spiritual matters, as she read her Bible regularly. It was not until age nineteen that I learned the reason the rainbow appeared in the sky, and this through her. Called the Noahic covenant, Genesis 9:13-15 states: "I set My rainbow in the cloud, and it shall be for the sign of the covenant between Me and the earth. It shall be, when I bring a cloud over the earth, that the rainbow shall be seen in the cloud; and I will remember My covenant which is between Me and you and every living creature of all flesh; the waters shall never again become a flood to destroy all flesh."

While she was not always able to answer all of my questions, I give her much credit for teaching me how God can sometimes work in our lives. One day while sitting in a nice restaurant, in the midst of our conversation, she made the remark "Maybe He will come." It was not until later that I realized she was referring to the Holy Spirit working through her to speak to me. What a special memory of her that I hold of that moment! It is absolutely amazing what a profound impact we can have on someone with less than a minute of time! During this period God did indeed speak to me through her about some critical issues in my life.

Around this same time the Good Lord also chose to get my attention through my Pastor, a true man of God. Due to a recent move (with the Lord leading me to Atlanta), I left that Church though I still talk to and visit with the Pastor. God also told me He would provide another man of God to instruct me through. God not only used this Pastor to grant me understanding but to inform me that I was called by Him as a prophet. I must admit, I went through a period wondering if this really was the Lord speaking to me as I know from personal experience the devil is such a deceiver. My God, being patient with me, did convince me without a shadow of a doubt it was indeed Him.

For many years prior to these events, I prayed diligently in my prayer closet. We learn in Galatians 6:9-10, "And let us not grow weary while doing good, for in due season we shall reap if we do not lose heart. Therefore, as we have opportunity, let us do good to all, especially to those who are of the household of faith." Jesus has told us in Matthew 6:6, "But you, when you pray, go into your room, and when you have shut your door, pray to your Father who is in the secret place, and your Father who sees in secret will reward you openly." That is precisely what God did with me over a number of years. He not only informed me of some future things to occur in my life but granted me some intense understanding of the Holy Scriptures (though not all of Scripture).

The fact that God used both my Grandmother and my Pastor as vessels to work through intrigued me and I know it is God's perfect way. God graciously and patiently rewarded me allowing me to ask many, many questions. He answered personal life questions and questions on deep theological subjects. I must tell you that I thoroughly enjoyed being able to do this and consider it a great honor. Ephesians 3:20 tells us one of the great Truths about our great God, "Now to Him who is able to do exceedingly abundantly above all that we ask or think, according to the power that works in us." Verse 21 continues "to Him be Glory in the Church by Christ Jesus to all generations, forever and ever. Amen." I know God is very capable to surprise you in an unexpected way if you use your prayer time wisely.

Now at this time I would like to point out a very important truth. I want you, the reader, to know if I was not absolutely certain of the facts that I will tell you that Almighty God confirmed, there is no way on God's green earth that I would dare publish them in a book. What I declare in the Name of Jesus if in fact is not true, I would be sealing my own death. In Deuteronomy 18:20 God has stated, "But the prophet who presumes to speak a word in My name, which I have not commanded him to speak, or who speaks in the name of others gods, that prophet shall die." The Lord spoke to me over years about many things and though I did not receive answers to all my questions, I tried very hard to make sure I understood correctly those that He did answer.

In Jeremiah 23:28 Jehovah has told us, "The prophet who has a dream, let him tell a dream; and he who has My word, let him speak My word faithfully." I was actually obeying God in this even before I was aware I was a prophet, which I find rather interesting. I certainly plan, with the Lords help, to spread the good news of that dream to the ends of the earth! Also the good news of salvation! Though called as a teacher years ago, being called as a prophet is still pretty new to me. I am truly amazed and greatly honored to be counted among the many prophets I have often admired over the years, and especially for "such a time as this." I have thought many times how special it must have been to have been living at the time Christ Jesus walked on earth as God in the flesh. I am very pleased to be able to proclaim His return in a mighty way! To be honest, I would not have guessed God would call me to this monumental task, but I wouldn't change it for the world!

Due to the verse of James 3:1, "My brethren, let not many of you become teachers, knowing that we shall receive a stricter judgment", I did not desire to become a teacher. However God had other plans as I was nominated and voted in at the Church I attended so quickly, I don't think I had the chance to turn it down! I realized it was God's choice for me and today I am very, very thankful. God Himself placed a deep desire in me to know the Holy Scriptures in depth. People have remarked that the Bible contradicts itself, and I admit at times it seems to, but when understood correctly Spiritually, we find it does not. In part of the verse of 2nd Peter 3:16, the Bible itself states "in which are some things hard to understand", these are some of those that God planted in my heart as a desire to know.

Why was I chosen by God to warn unbelievers of His return and to alert believers of our soon being gathered to Jesus? To answer the first part of that question, God has always given a warning in one way or another before bringing judgment. Even when He knows the unbeliever will not listen, He still sends someone. It is His nature which is love. In 1st John 4:8 we find out, "He who does not love does not know God, for God is love." And it only seems natural and right that the Good Lord would alert believers to the great return of the Lord Jesus. For those who choose to love, it will give them the opportunity to serve God above and beyond the call of duty. In Romans 12:1 we find what God expects of each and every Christian, "I beseech you therefore, brethren, by the mercies of God, that you present your bodies a living sacrifice, holy, acceptable to God, which is your reasonable service." So above and beyond the call of duty seems to require a great deal of effort. I believe Paul accomplished this along with a number of others over the years.

Now as far as me being called individually as a prophet to warn people of His return, well I just do not know. Perhaps it is because of my prayers over the years or possibly because God knew I would get the job accomplished, or maybe a combination of both. Whatever the reason I am very blessed to have been chosen and I will be praying, and covet your prayers, that I will pursue this call to the very best of my God-given ability.

For those of you not already involved in the work of God, I strongly urge you to get involved and earn some of those eternal rewards. If you are not sure what the work of God is, John 6:29 tells you, "This is the work of God, that you believe in Him whom He sent." This is a reference of God the Father sending His greatly beloved Son, Jesus Christ. And you should prayerfully ask God to show you what Church He wants you to be joined to (if you are not presently with one that teaches salvation through Christ and eternal salvation, that is, once saved, always saved). I want to point out that God does not just want us full-time but for all time!

It is clear to me that I will be honored around the world as Jesus has told us in Matthew 13:57, "A prophet is not without honor except in his own country and in his own house." Though I am a United states citizen, this does not refer to the entire country but the much smaller area where I am from. And though I have no doubt this is true, I believe without fail I will also be ridiculed and mocked by some. I am willing to endure this and the persecution which is certain to come.

In Deuteronomy 18:22 the Lord tells us, "When a prophet speaks in the name of the Lord, if the thing does not happen or come to pass, that is the thing which the Lord has not spoken; the prophet has spoken it presumptuously; you shall not be afraid of him." As mentioned earlier, in a later chapter I will clearly distinguish between what God told me to make known and my speculation on end time events. Also I am presently 51 years of age and have been divorced for 28 years. I have truly waited patiently on God to show/provide me with a wife. I struggled for years not knowing if it was permissible for me to remarry. And then when I found it was ok (my wife left and divorced me), I struggled with getting the right one. I asked God to show me and got to the point that I thought perhaps He intended for me to remain as I was. I told Him I would rather marry but would remain unmarried if that was His will.

I tell you this because the end time events I am revealing to you in this book are more than ten years in the future. However, among other things, the Lord has revealed to me that I will indeed marry and will have three children, two girls and a boy. So you can keep track to see if that comes to pass. I will also pray and ask God if He wishes to reveal other things to me that I will make known to you. I am sure that God is coming soon , and I have no doubt He wants you as a believer to have this confidence. Truly to God be the Glory!

Chapter 3
The Blessed Hope

It is commonly believed among many who consider themselves Evangelical Christians (the group I like to call 'Mainstream Christianity', those with the most correct beliefs), that the rapture could have happened since the days of the Apostles. I will attempt to convince the reader, with the Lord's help, that this is an incorrect conclusion about God's program.

There are numerous passages in the Bible that prove beyond a doubt the rapture could not possibly have happened during any generation since the time of Christ. The Lord told Peter in John 21:18, "Most assuredly, I say to you, when you were younger, you girded yourself and walked where you wished; but when you are old, you will stretch out your hands, and another will gird you and carry you where you do not wish." So Jesus prophesied here that the rapture could not occur until after Peter became old. As I stated earlier, all Christians will go up in the rapture. And there are several passages in the Book of Acts (23:11, 27:24) that also prove the rapture could not happen until after those things came to pass. Matthew

24:14 states, "And this gospel of the kingdom will be preached in all the world as a witness to all the nations, and then the end will come," has been cited to prove this fact but it can be successfully argued (in and of itself) that this could have happened in each generation. So if the rapture was not imminent (a theological term meaning 'about to happen') in Peter's day, which is clear, I am not aware of anything that has changed concerning prophecy (that is, that has yet to be fulfilled), from that time until, say, the early 1900s.

Rather, a prophetic event that had to happen before the rapture could occur, the re-birth of the nation of Israel in unbelief, is clearly shown in the 37th chapter of Ezekiel. Ezekiel 37:8 states, "Indeed, as I looked, the sinews and the flesh came upon them, and the skin covered them over; but there was no breath in them." The word breath is used in Scripture to refer to the Holy Spirit, which all Christians have in them, that is, God Himself! For almost 2000 years the Jews were a people without a nation. That changed on the historic day of May 14th, 1948, when the state of Israel was born. Though some have become believers in the Lord, as a nation they continue in unbelief.

At the end of that prophecy of Ezekiel

37:1-14, we learn that time of unbelief changes, "I will put My Spirit in you, and you shall live, and I will place you in your own land. Then you shall know that I the Lord, have spoken it and performed it, 'says the Lord.'" As of this writing there are approximately 7 million Jews now living in Israel with more joining their ranks regularly. The Great Tribulation, which will be discussed in more detail later, is described in Jeremiah 30:7, "Alas! For that day is great, so that none is like it; and it is the time of Jacob's trouble, but he shall be saved out of it." The mention of Jacob here is a reference to Israel because Jacob, who is the grandson of Abraham, fathered the beginning of the twelve tribes of Israel. In Zechariah 13:9 we are told by God, who knows the end from the beginning (Isaiah 46:10), "I will bring the one-third through the fire, will refine them as silver is refined, and test them as gold is tested. They will call on My name, and I will answer them. I will say 'This is My people'; and each one will say, "The Lord is my God'." So Israel will be saved as a nation during the last three and a half years of the then broken covenant period! They, in fact, will be the nation to reign on earth during the Millennial Reign of Christ.

One of the most compelling reasons (aside

from the fact that **Almighty** God told me of His imminent return), that the rapture could not have occurred in any generation before this one (after Peter's day as explained earlier), is the plain fact that it hasn't! In Scripture it is clearly outlined that there were prophecies not yet fulfilled and therefore the rapture could not have been about to happen as many claim today. It is a passage most often misunderstood, I think by many because of the incorrect view that the rapture will happen before the signing of the seven year covenant (this will be explained in more detail later).

In Paul's day the Thessalonians were concerned that the Day of the Lord, also called the Day of Christ, had already come. God lovingly through the Apostle Paul, set this false notion aright. And he told them what had to happen first before the rapture, and therefore the Day of the Lord, could occur. This is clear from 2nd Thessalonians 2:1-3, "Now, brethren, concerning the coming of our Lord Jesus Christ, and our gathering together to Him, we ask you, not to be soon shaken in mind or troubled, either by spirit or by word or by letter, as if from us, as though the Day of Christ had come. Let no one deceive you by any means; for that Day will not come unless the falling away comes first, and the man of sin is revealed, the son of perdition."

The phrase 'our gathering together to Him' is most definitely a reference to the rapture. And Paul, inspired by God, was clearly not telling them it was going to happen in their lifetimes, otherwise he would have been bearing false witness. He was without a doubt telling them (and us) that something had to happen before the rapture could come. Many think, as I once did, that the apostasy, the falling away prophesied in 2nd Thessalonians 2:3, would come about just before the signing of the seven year covenant, or possibly in the first three and a half years. I am of the opinion that we are experiencing this falling away in our present day.

Although the number going to Church is considerably higher in the United states, it has fallen to about half a percent in England! One only has to travel briefly (as I recently did) to see the religious heritage that once thrived there. And in Western Europe Church attendance is even lower by more than one hundred percent. These figures are no less than staggering!

For the sake of the younger believers and for some older 'babes' (and the many I hope will come to salvation after reading this book by paying attention to the hearing of the Word of God), I will attempt to give a basic overview of Biblical events that have already passed and some of those that are yet to come. In a later chapter, I will go into greater detail which I hope will intrigue the more mature believer. And a further hope is also to cause others to increase their Spiritual understanding and draw near to God. James 4:8 says, "Draw near to God and He will draw near to you. Cleanse your hands, you sinners: and purify your hearts, you double-minded." This is a call to unbelievers. And I will give the three major views of the rapture.

God created Adam and Eve in His image and in His likeness (Genesis 1:26). In Deuteronomy 6:4 (this is part of Israel's Shema) we are told, "Hear; O Israel: The Lord our God, the Lord is one!" Although the word Trinity is not found in Scripture, the concept clearly is. There is God the Father, God the Son (and the Son of God as well), and God the Holy Spirit, three separate "persons". From the last part of Revelation 1:4 we find, "and from the seven Spirits who are before His throne." And in Isaiah 11:2, God again tells us, "The Spirit of the Lord shall rest upon Him, the Spirit of wisdom and understanding, the Spirit of counsel and might, the Spirit of knowledge and of the fear of the Lord." So we learn that there are literally seven Spirits of God! Just as the three separate "persons" are together one Lord, the seven Spirits are together the Holy Spirit. In the Bible seven is the number of completion. The concept of the trinity is a difficult one to grasp but nevertheless true. They all agree with one another. The trinity can be seen in 1st John 5:7, "For there are three that bear witness in heaven: the Father, the Word, and the Holy Spirit; and these three are one." The word "Word" in this verse refers to Jesus who came to earth and dwelt among us (see John 1:1, 1:14)!

So God created man in His image and likeness with three parts, a body, soul and spirit. In the 1st Book of Thessalonians, verse 5:23 confirms this fact, "Now may the God of peace Himself sanctify you completely; and may your whole spirit, soul and body be preserved blameless at the coming of our Lord Jesus Christ."

God also created man and woman as wholesome and good creatures. That is, at first without a sinful nature but with the ability to sin. God also created His angels with the ability to sin though not all chose to do so. Lucifer, thought to be God's highest order of angelic creation (though Michael might have been created as Lucifer was), fell from his position by sinning in his heart. He became known as the devil, satan and other names.

In Ezekiel 28:12-15, satan is depicted as a king, a practice of fallen angels "ruling" over areas that is expressed more than once in Scripture. He is also seen as he was in his original perfect state. "Son of man, take up a lamentation for the king of Tyre, and say to him, 'Thus says the Lord God: "You were the seal of perfection, full of wisdom and perfect in beauty. You were in Eden, the garden of God; every precious stone was your covering; the sardius, topaz, and diamond, beryl, onyx, and jasper, sapphire, turquoise, and emerald with gold. The workmanship of your timbrels and pipes was prepared for you on the day you were created. You were the anointed cherub who covers; I established you; you were on the holy mountain of God; you walked back and forth in the midst of fiery stones. You were perfect in your ways from the day you were created, till iniquity was found in you.'"

As the age-old story goes, man and woman were in the Garden of Eden in their unfallen state and along comes the devil (depicted as a serpent in the Bible, see Genesis 3:1, also Revelation 12:9). He managed to deceive Eve who in turn led her husband into partaking of the forbidden fruit of the tree of the knowledge of good and evil. By this single evil act, satan amazingly plunged the entire human race into sin (and probably still proud of it). He managed to create a fourth part to God's wonderful creations called the "flesh" in Scripture. Every person born since has inherited this sinful nature through Adam from that fateful day. Please be sure to read chapter six of this book to find out how to overcome this tragic episode in the history of man.

Ever since, man has been in a struggle with good and evil. In the society I grew up in (and my guess is everyone else experienced this in one way or another), this battle of good versus evil could be seen in the movies as well as other areas of life. God and satan have been in a universal conflict with one another since his fall. This spiritual (though this includes physical at times) fight stretches from earth to the third heaven where God's very Throne is located. And the Holy Bible wonderfully explains that God and His people will come out the winners...forever! Though satan is no doubt powerful and worldwide, there is just no comparison there to God Himself. We are told in Matthew 4:10 when Jesus told the devil, "away with you satan! For it is written, 'You shall worship the Lord your God, and Him only you shall serve.'"

God has been trying everything He possibly could for nearly six thousand years to draw people to Himself. In the Old Testament He chose Israel as His special nation. God told Moses in Exodus 19:5-6a, "Now therefore, if you will indeed obey My voice and keep My covenant then you shall be a special treasure to Me above all people; for all the earth is Mine. And you shall be to Me a kingdom of priests and a holy nation." God desires both Jews and Gentiles to live with Him, a perfect Creator, without sin forever. Contrary to what some believe, the nation of Israel is still in God's plan. They will be ruling and reigning with Christ during the one thousand year reign to come on the earth. Also known as the Millennial Reign of Christ. Gentiles who accept Jesus as their Savior will be there as well.

God also sent His Old Testament saints, the prophets, to draw Israel to Himself so that they in turn could bring some Gentiles to Him. And He used other ways including Angels and Judges. In the New Testament He came Himself to earth in the flesh as was absolutely necessary. More on this later. Jesus, Christ in the flesh, chose Apostles to draw people (by God) out of the kingdom of darkness and put them in the KINGDOM OF LIGHT! He has since "hired" many, many laborers for His kingdom. He has literally "left no stone unturned" when it comes to salvation and will continue to do so until that final call.

The first sacrifice of His creation, God Himself made to cover the nakedness of Adam and Eve. Though there was nothing wrong with their nakedness in and of itself, after their fall because of their shame, the sacrifice became necessary to point to Christ. The many Old Testament sacrifices made by man all pointed to the essential one time sacrifice Jesus made on the Cross. After Jesus (God) came in the flesh and shed His precious blood on the Cross, necessary for the removal of sin, the sacrificial system was ended. Jesus literally paid it all forever! During the Millennial Reign, the sacrificing will begin again but I think not to point to Jesus, as the Old Testament sacrifices did, thereby appeasing God. It will most likely serve as a reminder of the

Jesus Really IS Coming Back.....Soon!

indescribable gift of Christ, something similar to our taking communion today.

There have been a little less than four thousand years since the birth of Christ and a little more than two thousand since. There have been just under six thousand in total (more on that fact later). God has been very patient waiting for many to come to repentance and accept Jesus as Savior. In 2nd Peter 3:9 we learn, "The Lord is not slack concerning His promise, as some count slackness, but is longsuffering toward us, not willing that any should perish but that all should come to repentance." A time is coming in the not to distant future when God will call His people to Himself. It is my hope that you, the reader, will be with us when Jesus descends with a shout, with the voice of an archangel and with the trumpet of God!

There is coming soon the signing of the seven year covenant with many by satan's man, the antiChrist. This is confirmed in the first part of Daniel 9:27, "Then he shall confirm a covenant with many for one week..." This will include Israel but may possibly, and seems to indicate to include other nations as well, perhaps in that area. In Scripture days are often used to mean years. This covenant will ensure Israel that they can build the fourth temple and begin their sacrificial system (they are presently either ready or very close to being ready) in peace and safety once again.

Although not found in Scripture, this seven year period is most often incorrectly labeled as the Tribulation. There is a Great Tribulation that is referred to in several places in Scripture but not a seven year period as such. I will go over some details now and more in a later chapter. Though the Great Tribulation period is most often considered as lasting three and a half years, I am of the opinion that this is incorrect as well. It seems best to distinguish between the Great Tribulation (by man and satanic activity) and the time of the wrath of God. Jesus told us in Matthew 24:21, "For then there will be Great Tribulation, such as has not been since the beginning of the world until this time, no, nor ever shall be." More on the Day of the Lord later.

There have been periods of tribulation brought on Jews and Gentiles alike for thousands of years by satan ("... the spirit who now works in the sons of disobedience", Ephesians 2:2b). However, during the Great Tribulation there will be horror beyond one's imagination, as we do not having anything to compare it to. It will be a time unparalleled in the history of man, the likes of which will never again be repeated. It will surpass the terrible times that have come on earth including the feared Assyrians flaying people alive by removing their skin all over. Also, the horrible times of the inquisition, Stalin's evil reign and the almost unbelievable horrendous times Hitler brought on the Jews known as the Holocaust. In Matthew 24:22 we are told, "And unless those days were shortened, no flesh would be saved; but for the elect's sake those days will be shortened." Almighty God will intervene!

During the first three and a half years of the covenant with death (Isaiah 28:18) there will be a period of false peace, at least for Israel. He, the antiChrist, will apparently guarantee their safety so they may perform their sacrifices without any worry from their Middle Eastern enemies or any other enemies. According to Daniel 9:27, he will break the covenant in the midst of the week and bring an end to sacrifice and offering.

In Revelation 12:7-8 the Bible states, "And war broke out in heaven: Michael and his angels fought with the dragon; and the dragon and his angels fought, but they did not prevail, nor was a place found for them in heaven any longer." Many think that this war has already taken place. In

Luke 10:18 Jesus said, "I saw satan fall like lightning from heaven." Even if Jesus was referring to this future war in that verse, keep in mind He was (and is) a Prophet. It is clear from Revelation 12:12 that close to two thousand years have not elapsed since the war but satan will have only a short time before he is bound for a thousand years. That verse states, "Therefore rejoice, O heavens, and you who dwell in them! Woe to the inhabitants of the earth and the sea! For the devil has come down to you, having great wrath, because he knows that he has a short time." He has fallen from his position and this occurred before he deceived Eve. It is clear from the Book of Job that he had access to heaven after this. When he is defeated and cast out of heaven, he will no longer be able to enter heaven. Satan, at this time still thinks, amazingly, that he can defeat the God of all gods, the Almighty! God did confirm that, he has deceived himself into believeing he can win.

It is feasible to believe that this war will occur at approximately the same time the "man of sin" breaks the treaty with Israel and ushers in the start of the Great Tribulation. The rapture will also occur around this general time-frame with both events likely to occur close together. The time of

God's wrath will begin just after the end of the tribulation. And the second coming of Christ to earth will happen very soon! For more clarification please refer to the chart and additional details in chapter five.

Although the Great Tribulation will have ended, many will gather together to fight against the Lord of lords and King of kings. In 2nd Thessalonians 2:8 we learn what will come of the beast: "...whom the Lord will consume with the breath of His mouth and destroy with the brightness of His coming." And in Revelation 19:20-21 we are given additional details, "Then the beast was captured, and with him the false prophet who worked signs in his presence, by which he deceived those who received the mark of the beast and those who worshiped his image. These two were cast alive into the lake of fire burning with brimstone. And the rest were killed with the sword which preceded from the mouth of Him who sat on the horse. And all the birds were filled with their flesh." The "Him" who sat on the horse refers to none other than Jesus!

Around this time, God deals with the devil but in a different sense than He did in the Book of Job. We are told in Revelation 20:1-3, "Then

I saw an angel coming down from heaven, having the key to the bottomless pit and a great chain in his hand. He laid hold of the dragon, that serpent of old, who is the devil and satan, and bound him for a thousand years; and he cast him into the bottomless pit, and shut him up, and set a seal on him, so that he should deceive the nations no more till the thousand years were finished. But after these things he must be released for a little while." The following will happen after the thousand years are over. God will allow him to deceive the nations once again and to gather them for battle. We find in Revelation 20:9-10, "They went up on the breadth of the earth and surrounded the camp of the saints and the beloved city. And fire came down from God out of heaven and devoured them. The devil, who deceived them, was cast into the lake of fire and brimstone where the beast and the false prophet are. And they will be tormented day and night forever and ever." Then the dead, small and great, will be judged at the Great White Throne Judgment after which God will create a new heaven and a new earth. The holy city, the New Jerusalem, will come down out of heaven where Christians will live with God throughout eternity. See the Book of Revelation for more details.

So Jesus will return to earth bodily with His saints (the angels will come at some point according to Matthew 24:31) and after destroying the beast and the others who attempt to defeat Him, He will judge the nations. Since Jesus is clearly in control at this time, it seems evident the one thousand year Millennial Reign of Christ has already begun. In Matthew 25:32-33 the Bible tells us, "All the nations will be gathered before Him, and He will separate them one from another, as a shepherd divides his sheep from the goats. And He will set the sheep on His right hand, but the goats on the left." We are further told that the goats (the unsaved) will have to leave the earth (by death). So the Millennial Kingdom at this point will only have believers as far as the human race is concerned. Those who are still in their natural bodies will repopulate the earth and those saints who returned with Christ will rule and reign with Him! We will be in our resurrected bodies and will be as the angels of heaven, not given in marriage and thus not involved in the repopulation of the earth. I so look forward to that time! Read your Bible or get one!

At this time I would like to relate briefly the three major views of the rapture. They are pretribulation, midtribulation and posttribulation. The most popular view is that of the pretribulationists. This view states that the Church will be caught away just prior to the signing of the seven year covenant by antiChrist with the many. Although the term itself is indeed correct, the timing is not as will be discussed later. The next view, that of the midtribulationists, will no doubt eventually become the most popular to be sure! The folks that hold this view believe the Church will be raptured in the first three and a half years of the seven year covenant. And the third view is that of the posttribulationists. They hold that the Church will go through the Great Tribulation and will be gathered to Jesus in the air just prior to His return. One thing everyone can agree on is that only one view is correct. I trust that I will be able to convince many before that time, which view, is in fact the right one.

One of the most supporting verses for those who hold the pretribulation view is Revelation 3:10. It states "Because you have kept My command to persevere, I also will keep you from the hour of trial which shall come upon the whole world; to test those who dwell on the earth." As mentioned earlier, the seven year covenant is most often incorrectly understood as being seven years of tribulation. And with the "hour of trial" relating to the seven years of tribulation, it is no wonder that this view is presently the most popular. In fact, that verse relates to the rapture as understood but with the understanding that we will be kept from the Great Tribulation which will occur in the last three and a half years.

The posttribulationists also use that same verse of Revelation to support their view. It is believed that the Greek construction in that verse allows the words "keep from" to have a different meaning than Jesus intended. They believe God will keep us from the horrors here on earth while still living here. While I think we may possibly experience more intense tribulation (the tribulation Christians can go through today) as we come closer to His return, we will most certainly not go into the Great Tribulation.

There will be more discussion in the next chapter about the correct view. Now I will explain why I chose to name this chapter "The Blessed Hope". One of the main verses used by those that believe the rapture could have happened in previous generations is Titus 2:13. It states, "looking for the blessed hope and glorious appearing of our great God and Savior Jesus Christ." The word "looking" is, I think, what leads them to believe it was possible for each generation to disappear from the earth. It seems to me that if I take the verse in that context, is to understand that God was deliberately setting up each preceding generation for disappointment. That just does not square with the God I know. Even if I was sure that the rapture would not happen for a hundred years, I could still view the "blessed hope" as just that! When I was younger, I tried to view the prospect of getting older in a positive light, that of getting closer to being with God. I rather believe that God has kept it secret in such a way that most, if they were completely honest, would have to admit they really didn't know when the rapture will occur. I am here to tell you it will be soon! To God be the Glory!

Chapter Four
Time of Return

The views that I will be explaining in this chapter, with one exception, have been around for years, just not widely accepted. They will tie in nicely together and it is my hope and prayer that the reader will give these strong consideration before making any decision against them. I am of the opinion as a teacher gifted by the Holy Spirit that they are correct.

In 2nd Peter 3:8 we are told, "But, beloved, do not forget this one thing, that with the Lord one day is as a thousand years, and a thousand years as one day." This no doubt teaches that God is eternal. Psalm 90:2 tells us, "Before the mountains were brought forth, or ever you had formed the earth and the world, even from everlasting to everlasting, You are God." God has no beginning and no ending, a Truth that is beyond my comprehension, but I accept it by faith.

Based on what the Lord revealed to me, I think that 2nd Peter 3:8 is a subtle hint by God of His planned program. There were six days of creation during which the Lord God made the earth and the heavens. In Genesis 2:1-2 the Bible tells us, "Thus the heavens and the earth, and all the host of them, were finished. And on the seventh day God ended His work which He had done and He rested on the seventh day from all His work which He had done." I believe that the six days of creation correspond to six thousand years of time man has on earth before the Millennial Reign. The one thousand year Reign of Christ seems to correspond to the day of rest. He is a perfect God and it is a perfect fit! Is God capable of completing a program such as this and still keep His promise? In 2nd Peter 3:9 we find, "The Lord is not slack concerning His promise, as some count slackness, but is longsuffering toward us, not willing that any should perish but that all should come to repentance." You better believe He can! He tells us in Jeremiah 32:27, "Behold, I am the Lord, the God of all flesh. Is there anything too hard for Me?" No answer for that rhetorical question needed!

There have been numerous theologians over the years who have calculated from Scripture the time from God creating Adam until their day. Probably the best known and most widely accepted of these is ArchBishop James Ussher (Usher) of Armagh. He came up with a date of 4004 B.C. (Before Christ) for the creation of Adam.

Now sadly, B.C. is listed in many books as B.C.E., standing for Before the Common Era. Although this date is close, it is off by approximately 25 years. Reference...Almighty God! More on this later.

It is at this time that I would like to point out you will not see any book or author references noted in the back of this book. Although I have read many fine books by many fine men of God, the Lord Himself is the One who gave me the understanding of these Truths. As mentioned earlier, I had either heard or read many of them before but it was God who confirmed many of them (and I believe He will confirm the others later). So it only seems fair to give Him all the Glory! I hope this is understandable.

Interestingly, a number of years ago, as the Providence of God would have it, I ran across a time line in a 1568 Geneva Bible that was completed to the year 1560. I will attempt to detail that time line at the end of this chapter and include a copy from a later 19th Century King James (it is more legible). I became rather amazed at this find as it put the six thousand mark about thirty-six years away! God later confirmed that this time line was close indeed!

I want you to keep in mind that over the course of many years, days and even months have been added or subtracted (to suit their various needs or wants), so only God Himself knows the precise time as far as I am aware. If we use some reasoning ability, with God's help, we are able to see what Jesus meant when He gave what is known as the Olivet Discourse of Matthew chapter 24 and Luke chapter 21.

Jesus told us in Matthew 24:36, "But of that day and hour no one knows, not even the angels of heaven, but My Father only." What day did Jesus mean, the day of the rapture or the day Christ touches down on planet earth? Well, in the following verse Jesus said, "But as the days of Noah were, so also will the coming of the Son of Man be." And in Matthew 24:15-31 Jesus explained events that will happen in the Great Tribulation just before His return. And in Matthew 24:33, the parable of the fig tree, He said, "So you also, when you (He was obviously referring to a future generation of believers) see all these things, know that it is near- at the doors." So just before and just after Matthew 24:36, Jesus was clearly referring to that "day and hour no one knows" as the day He will return to earth bodily. Theologians have often mistakenly taken Matthew 24:36 to refer to not having any clue about the general time frame of either the rapture or the second coming of Christ to earth. In conclusion, since they were told what to look for, it is without a doubt that they will not know the day or hour but will know that the bodily return of Jesus to earth is close. Now if they are allowed to know when it is close, it seems reasonably fair to assume that we as Christians are able to know now, and we are.

Many theologians (a term meaning student of God) have incorrectly taken Acts 1:7 to apply to all of the Christians in each generation. It states, "And He said to them, 'it is not for you to know times or seasons which the Father has put in His own authority.'" The New Testament was not written when Jesus made this statement, just before ascending to the Father. He spoke this directly to them and not to all Christians in all generations. God has, in one way or another, always warned before bringing judgment. He must, as it is His nature to express His love even when He knows not all will listen. Hebrews 13:8 says, "Jesus Christ is the same yesterday, today, and forever", so He surely will warn before His return. And He has specifically told me to warn of His imminent return! I believe this book is one of the best and quickest ways to accomplish that task. It will be put in audio form to reach the illiterate. I believe many will come to Christ as a result of hearing chapter six verbally.

Something to note is when Jesus rebuked the Pharisees and Sadducees for being able to determine the weather but not recognizing His visitation. In Matthew 16:3 Jesus said, "...Hypocrites! You know how to discern the face of the sky, but you cannot discern the signs of the times." Writings of prophecy have increased significantly in the last thirty years or so due to the demand and a general belief that His return is near. I will admit that although everything to me pointed to the nearness of His return, I was not sure just how close it was until God confirmed it. I felt it was close but just could not "put my finger on it."

Although we are told that only God the Father knows the day and hour, nowhere in Scripture are we clearly told that we will not know when it is certainly close (and it is!). Mark 13:32-37 has often been cited to support that we as Christians will not have a clue to that time. "But of that day and hour no one knows, not even the angels in heaven, nor the Son, but only the Father. Take heed, watch and pray; for you do not know when the time is." And we still don't know exactly but some of us know it is close! Verse 34 continues, "It is like a man going to a far country, who left his house and gave authority to his servants, and to each his work, and commanded the doorkeeper to watch. Watch therefore, for you do not know when the master of the house is coming-in the evening, at midnight, at the crowing of the rooster, or in the morning-lest, coming suddenly, he find you sleeping. And what I say to you, I say to all: Watch!"

I glean several things from this previous set of passages. One is the emphasis on the more precise time, the hour that it will occur within a twenty-four hour period. Also an emphasis on watching. In those days the watchman would stand on the wall or in a tower on a constant lookout for someone approaching. This indicates that we will know ahead of time (and some of us do!) . And finally a warning to "take heed" so that you are not caught unaware. As is often the case, when someone says something to us, we are able to take it two different ways. And this is one of the reasons there is often a misunderstanding with the Scriptures. To be absolutely sure of the correct understanding, we must rely on the Lord for direction and not on our own powers of reasoning (though He sometimes allows our Spiritual understanding through these means with His help). John 14:26 tells us, "But the Helper, the Holy Spirit, whom the Father will send in My name, He will teach you all things, and bring to your remembrance all things that I said to you."

There is also one very important verse in the Bible that indicates we are to recognize the second coming of Christ when it is near. Hebrews 10:25 tells us, "not forsaking the assembly of ourselves together as is the manner of some, but exhorting one another, and so much the more as you see the Day approaching." Without a doubt this is a reference to the Day of the Lord which begins with the wrath of God toward the end of the seven year period of the covenant. There are numerous Days of the Lord spoken about in Scripture but this is the only one yet unfulfilled. I will discuss my conclusion about the timing of this Day in the next chapter on the Chronological Order of Events so "stay tuned"! The Day of the Lord begins with the wrath of God and goes through the thousand year

Reign of Christ and includes God creating the new heaven and new earth. We find in 2nd Peter 3:10, "But the day of the Lord will come as a thief in the night, in which the heavens will pass away with a great noise, and the elements will melt with fervent heat; both the earth and the works that are in it will be burned up." Although this verse has often been cited to show that we will not have any idea as to the timing of the rapture, there is a verse of Scripture that makes it abundantly clear this is not true. In 1st Thessalonians 5:4 we are told, "But you, brethren, are not in darkness, so that this Day should overtake you as a thief." It will come as a thief on the unbelieving but is not to do this to Christians.

I realize I will be repeating myself on numerous issues but I believe this will be helpful to many readers. These are, no doubt, complicated events that can be difficult to follow, particularly in chronological order. With God's help, if He is willing, we can do it!

God gave us the canon of Scripture and it is my understanding that at some point, at least some of us will be granted full knowledge of the Bible. I do believe it is God's will but not confirmed as such. Either way, To God Be The Glory!

Time Line

This is the time line I discovered in the back of a Geneva Bible printed in fifteen sixty-eight. It was first printed in the first Geneva edition of fifteen sixty. I have no doubt this discovery was not accidental but in the plan of God. He did tell me it was close to being correct! I will update the words to modern spelling but will keep the years the same.

From Adam unto the flood of Noah's day, there are one thousand six hundred and fifty-six years. For when Adam was one hundred and thirty years old, Seth was born. When Seth was one hundred and five years old, Enosh was born. When Enosh was ninety years old, Cainan was born. When Cainan was seventy years old, Mahalalel was born. When Mahalalel was sixty-five years old, Jared was born. When Jared was one hundred and sixty-two years old, Enoch was born. When Enoch was sixty-five years old, Methuselah was born. When Methuselah was one hundred and eighty-seven years old, Lamech was born. When Lamech was one hundred and eighty-two years old, Noah was born. According to Genesis 7:11, Noah was six hundred years old at the coming of the flood. The total of these years are one thousand six hundred and fifty-six years.

From the flood of Noah's day unto the departing of Abraham from Chaldea, there are three hundred and sixty-three years and ten days. For the flood continued for one year and ten days. Through Shem, who was Noah's son, Arphaxad was born two years after the flood. When Arphaxad was thirty-five years old Salah was born. When Salah was thirty years old, Eber was born. When Eber was thirty-four years old, Peleg was born. When Peleg was thirty years old, Reu was born. When Reu was thirty-two years old, Serug was born. When Serug was thirty years old, Nahor was born. When Nahor was twenty-nine years old, Terah was born. When Terah was seventy years old, Abraham was born. And Abraham departed from Chaldea when he was seventy years old. The total of these years is three hundred and sixty-three and ten days.

From Abraham departing from Ur of the Chaldeans unto the departing of the children of Israel from Egypt, there are four hundred and thirty years. Abraham was in Haran five years and departed when he was seventy-five years old. When Abraham was one hundred years old, Isaac was born. When Isaac was sixty years old, Jacob was born. Jacob went into Egypt with all his family when he was one hundred and thirty years old. Israel was in Egypt two hundred and twenty years. And Moses was eighty years old when led Israel out of Egypt. If we reduce the four hundred and thirty years by the two hundred and twenty years of Egyptian bondage and the eighty years of Moses' age, that leaves one hundred and thirty years. These one hundred thirty years are divided between Amram and Kohath. When Kohath was sixty-seven years old, Amram was born. When Amram was fifty-six years old, Moses was born. And when Moses was eighty years of age, he departed with the Israelites from Egypt. This accounts for the four hundred and thirty years found in Exodus 12:41 and in Galatians 3:17.

From the going forth of the Israelites from Egypt unto the building of the first Temple, there are four hundred and eighty years, as outlined in the following. Moses remained in the desert or wilderness for forty years. Joshua and Othneil ruled for forty years, Aioth (Ehud?) for seventy years, Deborah for forty years, Gideon forty years, Abimelech three years, Tela twenty-three years, Jair twenty-two years. Then they were without a judge for eighteen years until Jephthah came to rule. Jephthah ruled for six years, Ibzan for seven years, Elan for ten years, Abdon for eight years, Samson twenty years, Eli was judge and Priest for four years, Samuel and Saul reigned forty years, David was king forty years. Solomon began building the Temple in the fourth year of his reign.

From the building of the first Temple unto the captivity of Babylon there are four hundred and nineteen and a half years. Solomon reigned thirty-six years, Rehoboam seventeen years, Abijam three years, Asa forty-one years, Jehoshaphat twenty-five years, Jehoram eight years, Ahaziah one year, Athaliah the Queen seven years, Joash forty years, Amaziah twenty years, Uzziah fifty-two years, Jotham sixteen years, Ahaz sixteen years, Hezekiah twenty-nine years, Manasseh fifty-five years, Amon two years, Josiah thirty-one years, Jehoahaz three months, Eliacim (Zedekiah) eleven years, Jehoiachin three months.

Jerusalem was rebuilt one hundred and forty-three years after the Babylonian captivity. The captivity continued for seventy years. The children of Israel were delivered and had their freedom restored in the first year of Cyrus. They began building the Temple in the second year of Cyrus and finished in the forty-sixth year, which was the sixth year of Darius. After Darius reigned twenty years, Nehemiah was freed and went to build the city, which was finished in the thirty-second year of Darius. All the years from the building the Temple are twenty-six years. The total of years amounts to one hundred and forty-three.

From the restoration of the city unto the coming of Christ are four hundred and eighty-three years. It is mentioned in the ninth chapter of Daniel that Jerusalem should be built up again, and from that time unto the coming of Christ, there are sixty-nine weeks, with every week considered as seven years. So this totals to four hundred and eighty-three years. From the thirty-second year of Darius unto the forty-second year of Augustus, in which our Savior Christ was born, are just and complete. We calculate that from Adam unto Christ there are three thousand nine hundred and seventy-four years, six months and ten days. And from the birth of Christ unto this present year is fifteen hundred and sixty. Then the total number of years from the beginning of the world unto this present year of our Lord is five thousand five hundred thirty-four years, six months and ten days.

As I mentioned in chapter four, God confirmed that the above time line is close. However

I need to point out an error in the total they have given. Aioth (which apparently they meant Ehud) is listed as having judged for seventy years. According to Judges 3:30, "...the land had rest for eighty years." And Eli is shown as judging for forty-four years. According to 1st Samuel 4:18, "...And he had judged Israel forty years." These were likely just printing errors which were certainly not uncommon in that day.

We actually have quite a variety of time reckonings out there. And without God's help one can easily get very frustrated. The Jewish calendar is presently at five thousand seven hundred sixty-nine. This will leave about two hundred and thirty-one years to complete six thousand years. According to Usshers calculations we are presently in the six thousand and thirteenth year since the world was created. In the first time line, with corrections and by accepting the commonly accepted date of five eighty-six B.C. for the Babylonian captivity, one can come within thirty-six years of six thousand. Whether it is an important matter such as this or otherwise, I prefer to do as King David did as he wrote Psalm 20:7: "Some trust in chariots, and some in horses; But we will remember the name of the Lord our God"!

God did tell me He was in a hurry and I am certain that my hurry is faster than His. He did tell me the first time line is close and that the return of Christ is "at the steps" of the Church. I think He put it that way because of the Words of Jesus in Matthew 24:33, "So you also, when you see all these things, know that it is near-at the doors!" The Lord and I had quite a lengthy conversation on many Sundays over the years and I hope to remember additional information to share with you at a later date! To God Be The Glory!

A CHRONOLOGICAL INDEX

OF THE
YEARS AND TIMES FROM ADAM UNTO CHRIST,

PROVED BY

THE SCRIPTURES,

FROM THE COLLECTION OF DIVERS AUTHORS.

THE SUM OF THE YEARS OF THE FIRST AGE.

FROM Adam unto Noah's flood, are years 1656.
For when Adam was 130 years old, he begat Seth.
Seth being 105 years, begat Enos.
Enos being 90 years, begat Cainan.
Cainan being 70 years, begat Mahalaleel.
Mahalaleel being 65 years, begat Jared.
Jared being 162 years, begat Enoch.
Enoch being 65 years, begat Methuselah.
Methuselah at the age of 187, begat Lamech.
Lamech being 182 years, begat Noah.
Noah, at the coming of the flood, was 600 years old, as appeareth in the 7th of Genesis.
The whole sum of the years are 1656.

FROM the said flood of Noah, unto Abraham's departing from Chaldea, were 422 years and 10 days.
For the said flood continued one whole year, and ten days.
Shem (which was Noah's son) begat Arphaxad two years after that.
Arphaxad begat Salah when he was 35 years old.
Salah being 30 years old, begat Eber.
Eber at the age of 34, begat Peleg.
Peleg being 30 years, begat Reu.
Reu being 32 years, begat Serug.
Serug being 30 years, begat Nahor.
Nahor being 29 years, begat Terah.
Terah being 130 years, begat Abram.
And Abraham departed from Chaldea when he was 70 years old.
These said years accounted are 422 years and 10 days.

FROM Abraham's departing from Ur in Chaldea unto the departing of the children of Israel, are 430 years, gathered as followeth:—
Abraham was in Charran five years, and departed in the 75th year.
He begat Isaac when he was 100 years old, and in the 25th year of his departing.
Isaac begat Jacob when he was 60 years old.
Israel was in Egypt 220 years, which remain from that time.
Then deduct 90 years from this; for so old was Moses when he conducted the Israelites from Egypt.

So the rest of the years, that is to say 130, are divided between Amram and Chath.
Then Chath begat Amram at the age of 67 years.
Amram being 65 years begat Moses, who, in the 80th year of his age, departed with the Israelites from Egypt.
So this chronology is the 430 years mentioned in the 12th of Exodus, and the 3d to the Galatians.

FROM the going up of the Israelites from Egypt, unto the first building of the Temple, are 480 years, after this chronology and account.
Moses remained in the desert or wilderness, 40 years.
Joshua and Othniel ruled 40 years.
Ehud, 80 years.
Deborah, 40 years.
Gideon, 30 years.
Abimelech, 3 years.
Tola, 23 years.
Jair, 22 years.
Then they were without a captain, until the 18th year of Jephthah.
Jephthah, 6 years.
Ibzan, 7 years.
Elon, 10 years.
Abdon, 8 years.
Samson, 20 years.
Heli, judge and priest, 44 years.
Samuel and Saul reigned 40 years.
David was king 40 years.
Solomon in the 4th year of his reign, began the building of the temple.
These are the 480 years mentioned in the first book of Kings, ch. vi.

FROM the first building of the temple, unto the captivity of Babylon, are 419 years and an half.
Solomon reigned yet 36 years.
Rehoboam, 17 years.
Abijah, 3 years.
Asa, 41 years.
Jehoshaphat, 25 years.
Jehoram, 8 years.
Ahaziah, 1 year.
Athaliah the queen, 7 years.
Joash, 40 years.
Amaziah, 29 years.
Uzziah, 52 years.
Jehoahaz, 16 years.
Ahaz, 16 years.
Hezekiah, 29 years.
Manasses 55 years.
Amon, 2 years.
Josiah, 31 years.
Jehoaz, 3 months.
Eliakim, 11 years.
Jehoiachin, Jechonias, 3 months.
And here beginneth the captivity of Babylon.
The sum of these years are 419.

JERUSALEM was re-edified and built again after the captivity of Babylon, 70 years.
The captivity continued 70 years.
The children of Israel were delivered and restored to their freedom in the first year of Cyrus.
The temple was begun to be built in the second year of the said Cyrus, and finished in the 46th year, which was the 6th year of Darius. After that Darius had reigned 20 years, Nehemiah was restored to liberty and went to build the city, which was finished in the 32d year of the said Darius.
All the years from the building of the temple again are 68 years.
The whole sum of years amount to 70.

FROM the re-edifying of the city unto the coming of Christ are 483 years, after the chronology. It is mentioned in the 9th of Daniel, that Jerusalem should be built up again, and that from that time unto the coming of Christ, are 69 weeks, and every week is reckoned for seven years. So 69 weeks amount to 483 years; for, from the 32d year of Darius, unto the 42d year of Augustus, in which year our Saviour Christ was born, are just and complete so many years, whereupon we reckon, that from Adam unto Christ, are 3974 years, 3 months, and 10 days; and from the birth of Christ unto this present year, is 1834.
Then the whole sum and number of years, from the beginning of the world unto this present year of our Lord God, 1834, are just 5808 years, 6 months, and the said 10 days.

Chapter Five
Chronological Order of Events

It is without question that the events I am writing about in this chapter are difficult to follow. To put them in a chronological order that satisfies all the references in Scripture, is in my opinion, quite a task. I mention this because I know that many fine men of God, who have studied the Bible longer than me, have attempted to put the events in the correct order. I think we can agree that whether one studies for five years or fifty years, until God allows us to understand the Scriptures, it just will not happen. Although I have not read before about the order of events as I will expound them here, they do seem correct according to what God has confirmed to me. I will offer some views I am certain of and will also offer a bit of speculation. God just does not want us to know all the details at times. I desire your careful consideration and want to point out that I was gifted by the Holy Spirit not only as a prophet but also as a teacher. To my surprise, God told me I would "teach like no other." To God be the Glory!

I will begin with what is commonly known among Bible students as the seventy weeks of

Daniel. In Daniel 9:24 we learn, "Seventy weeks are determined for your people and for your holy city, to finish the transgression, to make an end of sins, to make reconciliation for iniquity, to bring in everlasting righteousness, to seal up vision and prophecy, and to anoint the Most Holy." The seventy weeks are divided in Scripture into three distinct periods of time. They are seven weeks, sixty-two weeks and the final week which will be discussed in great detail. With each week representing seven years, we have a period of forty-nine years, four hundred and thirty-four years and then the final seven years. This is a total of four hundred and ninety years.

The first two time periods have already passed, a total of four hundred and eighty-three years and we are awaiting the fulfillment of the final seven years. In Daniel 9:25 we learn, "Know therefore and understand, that from the going forth of the command to restore and build Jerusalem until Messiah the Prince, there shall be seven weeks and sixty-two weeks; the street shall be built again, and the wall, even in troublesome times." Then in the first part of Daniel 9:26 we see, "And after sixty-two weeks Messiah shall be cut off, but not for Himself..."

Whether one reckons the sixty-nine weeks by the Jewish or Gregorian Calendars, the same number of days can be calculated. The Jewish Calendar using three hundred sixty days per year, as does the Bible, when multiplied by the four hundred and eighty-three years, gives us one hundred and seventy-three thousand eight hundred and eighty days.

It is believed that the "command" of Daniel 9:25 was decreed by Artaxerxes Longimanus on March fifth, four hundred and forty-four B.C. (see Nehemiah 2:1-8). And Messiah was "cut off" (Daniel 9:26), at His Triumphal Entry into Jerusalem (He was crucified later that week), when He officially presented Himself as the Messiah, on March thirtieth, thirty-three A.D. After calculating the correct number of years and adding in the leap years days, and the extra days of March, one can come up with the same exact number of days. The Gregorian Calendar uses three hundred and sixty-five days per year. There are numerous books available if one desires to study this in further detail.

This brings us to the final week yet to be fulfilled spoken about in the first part of Daniel 9:27. God has told us, "Then he shall confirm a covenant with many for one week..." I shall now try to explain why it seems best not to view the entire week (or seven years) as one of complete tribulation.

First, just the fact that he confirms a covenant, does not constitute an act of "war" but more of a "peaceful" time of protection. At least for the "many" of Daniel 9: 27. Though I have no doubt, since the devil will not yet be bound, there will be an increase in the type of tribulation/persecution that Christians (who try to live in a Godly manner) experience today. In 2nd Timothy 3:12-13 we find, "Yes, and all who desire to live Godly in Christ Jesus will suffer persecution. But evil men and imposters will grow worse and worse, deceiving and being deceived."

Next, just as there are places in the world experiencing war with the majority of nations not engaging in battle, this seems to be the period Jesus described in Matthew 24:6 just prior to the Great Tribulation. He said, "And you will hear of wars and rumors of wars..."

I guess the most compelling point for me is the fact that the "man of sin" will break the covenant in the middle of the week. Daniel 9:27 tells us, "...But in the middle of the week he shall bring an end to sacrifice and offering..." As will be outlined in more detail later, this I am certain, is about the time when the Church is in heaven and Jesus is beginning to open the seven seals. And Revelation 6:4 tells us, "Another horse, fiery red, went out. And it was granted to the one who sat on it to take peace from the earth, and that people should kill one another; and there was given to him a great sword." So in conclusion, the first three and a half years, in general, will reflect more peaceful times in areas, as we have today. Now we are, of course, in a war on terror but it is not wide spread destruction as will happen in the Great Tribulation to occur in the last three and a half years.

With that established, I would like to go over an event I believe will begin in the first three and a half years. It is common for expositors to place the entire testimony of the two witnesses of Revelation 11 in the last half of the covenant. It is probably due to the fact that the length of their testimony matches that period. God has told us in Revelation 11:3, "And I will give power to my two witnesses, and they will prophesy one thousand two hundred and sixty days, clothed in sackcloth." But we find in Revelation 11 that after the witnesses are killed, they ascend into heaven and a great earthquake occurs, and that the third woe is yet to come, though it will come quickly, according to Revelation 11:14. We are not told how much time it will take for the seven angels to pour out the bowls of the wrath of God on the earth. And the gathering together of the forces to Armageddon has yet to occur as well. So it seems clear that the two witnesses will begin their testimony in the first half of the covenant. Perhaps this is why the beast will break his covenant with the many.

Another common practice of expositors is to see the saints given into the hands of the beast in the last three and a half years. We are told in Daniel 7:25, referring to the beast, "He shall speak pompous words against the Most High, shall persecute the saints of the Most High, and shall intend to change times and law. Then the saints shall be given into his hand for a time and times and half a time." The "time" is understood as a year, "times" as two years and "half a time" as six months or a total of three and a half years. And in Daniel 11:36 (seen as also referring to the beast), the Bible tells us, "Then the king shall do according to his own will; he shall exalt and magnify himself above every god, shall speak blasphemies against the God of gods, and shall prosper till the wrath has been accomplished; for what has been determined shall be done." I can see how this could be understood to refer to the giving of the saints into his hand for the last half of the covenant. However, for several reasons, I will try to show why I believe this is not correct.

First, when we compare two verses, they seem to be referring to the same period in God's program. We find in Matthew 24:29, "Immediately after the tribulation of those days the sun will be darkened, and the moon will not give its light; the stars will fall from heaven, and the powers of the heavens will be shaken." And in Revelation 6:12-14 we are told, "I looked when He opened the sixth seal, and behold, there was a great earthquake; and the sun became black as sackcloth of hair, and the moon became like blood. And the stars of heaven fell to the earth, as a fig tree drops its late figs when it is shaken by a mighty wind. Then the sky receded as a scroll when it is rolled up, and every mountain and island was moved out of its place." Though there is more information in the Revelation passage, there are enough similarities to ascertain they are referring to the same event.

Now, while some of the Book of Revelation is without a doubt not in chronological order, there is enough to aid us (with God's help of course) in determining most, if not all, of the correct order of events. It is clear that the opening of the seals by Jesus (the only One found worthy!) along with the trumpet and bowl judgments are all in chronological order, coming about one after another until their completion. Since the opening of the sixth seal precedes the rest of the judgments, and we are told in Matthew that the tribulation (by man and satanic activity) ended, I have come to a conclusion now to be outlined.

In Luke 4:18-19, the Lord has revealed to us, "The Spirit of the Lord is upon Me, because He has anointed Me to preach the gospel to the poor; He has sent Me to heal the brokenhearted, to proclaim liberty to the captives and recovery of sight to the blind, to set at liberty those who are oppressed; to proclaim the acceptable year of the Lord." It is accepted that this quotation of Jesus' Words, prophesied in the Book of Isaiah 61:1-2, which includes "And the day of vengeance of our God", includes a break until fulfillment presently of nearly two thousand years!

What I propose is that there is a break in time, albeit much shorter, between Matthew 24:29 (mentioned above) and Matthew 24:30, "Then the sign of the Son of Man will appear in heaven, and then all the tribes of the earth will mourn, and they will see the Son of Man coming on the clouds of heaven with power and great glory." After the Great Tribulation period is over toward the end of the seven year covenant, the wrath of God will begin. This is clear as after the opening of the sixth seal, as we see in Revelation 6:12, we then find in Revelation 6:15-17, "And the kings of the earth, the great men, the rich men, the commanders, the mighty men, every slave and every free man, hid themselves in the caves and in the rocks of the mountains, and said to the mountains and rocks, fall on us and hide us from the face of Him who sits on the throne and from the wrath of the Lamb! For the great day of His wrath has come, and who is able to stand?" And in Revelation 8:1 we are told, "When He opened the seventh seal, there was silence in heaven for about half an hour." This seems to indicate that something of great significance is to follow. So it seems best to consider the Day of the Lord as beginning with the seven trumpet judgments.

When we compare Matthew 24:29, Revelation 6:12-14 and Joel 2:30-31, we can come to a correct understanding of the order of at least most of these events in Scripture. Joel 2:30 tells us, "And I will show wonders in the heavens and in the earth: blood and fire and pillars of smoke. The sun shall be turned into darkness, and the moon into blood, BEFORE (emphasis mine) the coming of the great and awesome Day of the Lord." From Matthew 24:29 we see the Great Tribulation ends, and from Revelation 6:12-14, the opening of the sixth seal with people realizing the time of the wrath of the Lamb has come. Then in Revelation 8:1 we see the opening of the seventh seal with the trumpet and bowl judgments to follow. From Joel 2:31, the Day of the Lord begins following the events of Matthew 24:29.

Since we saw in Daniel 11:36, "...and shall prosper till the wrath has been accomplished...", some theologians, commonly understanding this as referring to the beast, have also placed all of the beast's wicked activities in the final three and a half years. However, in Revelation 9:5, previously established as part of God's wrath, God has told us, "And they were not given authority to kill them, but to torment them for five months." Counting this time along with the other judgments, I estimate God's wrath will last about six months.

And because the end of the Great Tribulation is seen as occurring prior to God's wrath, and yet the saints are given into the beast's hands for a "time and times and half a time" (again three and a half years), I see a different view (due to what the Lord revealed to me). It seems best to see the saints as being given into his hands approximately three years after the signing of the covenant, though only in part. Perhaps many saints will be martyred as they are today in certain areas. And it seems best to take the view that he will not have total control until after the beginning of the Great Tribulation in the second half of the now broken covenant. This is the time when it is clear he will have complete control over the saints lives (their bodies that is), and many will be killed. It is also clear that some will escape out of his hands, and live to repopulate the earth in the Millennial Reign. This is understood from the judgment of the nations found in Matthew 25:41-46. This helps us to understand how it is plausible for the saints to be "in his hands" in part of the first half of the covenant and yet not have the domination he will have in the second half.

Although the Lord did not tell me the exact time we would be raptured in the first three and a half years, He did indicate it would be toward the end of the first half of the covenant. I can put forth some speculation with several reasons for this, and why it may actually be very close to the midpoint.

Jesus said in John 9:4, "I must work the works of Him who sent Me while it is day; the night is coming when no one can work." This is probably referring to the period of time just prior to the second coming of Christ. After God has spent thousands of years and everything in His great power to draw people to Himself, can you imagine His wrath at being greatly hindered from showing His Great Love?

Knowing that the return of Christ is close will, I hope, cause many to minister with a fervency such as they have never done before. And hopefully some new converts will choose to become "laborers into His harvest." For God to give many this opportunity seems to me to be in line with His Holy Nature.

I believe that Daniel 12:1, "At that time Michael shall stand up, the great prince who stands watch over the sons of your people; and there shall be a time of trouble, such as never was since there was a nation,...", is a reference to the rapture and the beginning of the Great Tribulation. Michael, I am of the opinion, is the angel of 1st Thessalonians 4:16, "For the Lord Himself will descend from heaven with a shout, with the voice of an archangel, and with the trumpet of God. And the dead in Christ will rise first." Then we see in verses 17-18, "Then we who are alive and remain shall be caught up together with them in the clouds to meet the Lord in the air. And thus we shall always be with the Lord. Therefore comfort one another with these words." These are some of my favorite Scripture verses!

What I propose is that very close to the middle of the covenant or even in the middle, a series of events will occur. The antiChrist will break the covenant, the rapture will occur just beforehand (perhaps prodding him to break it) or just after. And while we are in the air, the war of Revelation 12:7 will be going on. Michael will probably shout something that will cause satan (and his angels) to go to war with Michael (and his assigned angels) in heaven. We see in Revelation 12:7-8, "And war broke out in heaven: Michael and his angels fought with the dragon; and the dragon and his angels fought, but they did not prevail, nor was a place found for them in heaven any longer." While some believe this war has already happened, when we look at Revelation 12:12, it becomes clear that it has not. "Therefore rejoice, O heavens, and you who dwell in them! Woe to the inhabitants of the earth and the sea! For the devil has come down to you, having great wrath because he knows that he has a short time." This "short time" seems to mean the time of the Great Tribulation and the wrath of God, and not the nearly two thousand years since the time of Jesus. It does seem feasible that these events occur very close to one another and then the Great Tribulation will begin. Aside from the war in heaven, I just do not see why Jesus would take us in the air instead of directly to heaven.

There is another event in Scripture that may be considered as supporting this series of events. Interestingly, the departure of the woman of Revelation 12 is mentioned twice. In Revelation 12:6, God has revealed to us, "Then the woman fled into the wilderness, where she has a place prepared by God, that they should feed her there one thousand two hundred and sixty days." Then in Revelation 12:13-14 we find, "Now when the dragon saw that he had been cast to the earth, he persecuted the woman who gave birth to the male child. But the woman was given two wings of a great eagle, that she might fly into the wilderness to her place, where she is nourished for a time and times and half a time, from the presence of the serpent." One can conclude that this particular "time and times and half a time" (twelve hundred and sixty days or three and a half years), does occur in the last half of the seven year covenant. It is likely that the war in heaven will occur just prior to this and this supports the view that the events will occur rapidly and close to the middle of the covenant.

Though I am going back and forth through the seven year covenant, toward the end of this chapter, I will put everything in order as I understand it will probably occur. Daniel's visions of chapter seven is partially explained in 7:23-24. "Thus he said: 'The fourth beast shall be a fourth kingdom on earth, which shall be different from all other kingdoms, and shall devour the whole earth, trample it and break it in pieces. The ten horns are ten kings who shall arise from this kingdom. And another shall rise after them; he shall be different from the first ones, and shall subdue three kings.'" These are, at least in time, a different set of kings than those we are told about in Revelation 17:12, "The ten horns which you saw are ten kings who have received no kingdom as yet, but they receive authority for one hour as kings with the beast." They are probably some of the same kings of Daniel 7:23-24, as he only subdued three.

It is also commonly believed among Bible students that the fourth kingdom (described as a beast) of Daniel 2:40 and 7:23 is a revival of the Roman Empire. And that the ten kings of Daniel chapter seven will come into power in the area of the former Roman Empire. I am not aware of any Scripture verse to indicate when this will occur, but I will guess it will be not too long before the signing of the seven year covenant. The antiChrist will somehow come into power, apparently peaceably (gleaned from Daniel 8:25). And perhaps politically to enable him to "confirm the covenant with many." Daniel 8:25 tells us "Through his cunning he shall cause deceit to prosper under his rule; and he shall exalt himself in his heart. He shall destroy many in their prosperity. He shall even rise against the Prince of princes; but he shall be broken without human means." This is a clear reference to the antiChrist rising against Jesus.

We are told in Revelation 3:10, "Because you have kept My command to persevere, I also will keep you from the hour of trial which shall come upon the whole world, to test those who dwell on the earth." This is most often understood to mean that the Lord will rapture the Church before the Great Tribulation. This is correct and, as shown earlier, this will be toward the end of the first three and a half years.

In Revelation 4:1 we find, "After these things I looked, and behold, a door standing open in heaven. And the first voice which I heard was like a trumpet, speaking with me, saying, 'Come up here, and I will show you things which must take place after this.'" This is believed to be a reference to the rapture. While this does seem to hint at our gathering to Jesus, there is an even more sure reference following closely after. Revelation 4:4 states, "Around the throne were twenty-four thrones and on the thrones I saw twenty-four elders sitting, clothed in white robes; and they had crowns of gold on their heads." These are some of the redeemed, now in heaven, who, at least part of, belong to the Church (confirmed by God). It seems likely that they include Old Testament saints as well. Apparently they have appeared before the judgment seat of Christ, as evidenced by the crowns on their heads.

The redeemed are still in heaven when we are told about the only One found worthy of opening the scroll. Revelation 5:5 tells us, "But one of the elders said to me, "Do not weep. Behold, the Lion of the tribe of Judah, the Root of David, has prevailed to open the scroll and to loose its seven seals."

Since chapters four, five, six are in chronological order apparently, this also supports a rapid succession of events around the midst of the covenant. In fact, the rapture, the breaking of covenant and the war in heaven, could in reality occur within a week or even less.

What I see could easily happen and seems to fit with Scripture is the rapture taking place, following with the war in heaven, with satan inspiring the "man of sin" to break the covenant. It does seem that at least the rapture and the war in heaven will take place very close to the middle of the covenant. And this would correspond to the woman (Israel) being nourished by God in the wilderness for three and a half years, the last half of the covenant period (see Revelation 12:14).

However, due to Daniel 12:11-12, "And from the time that the daily sacrifice is taken away, and the abomination of desolation is set up, there shall be one thousand two hundred and ninety days. Blessed is he who waits, and comes to the one thousand three hundred and thirty-five days", a little different timing could occur. On the previous view, that of the breaking of the covenant within a week's time, would mean the cleansing of the temple (of the abomination of desolation) would probably occur weeks after Christ returns to earth. Another guess is the covenant will be broken by the beast around thirty days before the precise middle of the covenant which is twelve hundred and sixty days. This because it seems the Lord would desire to cleanse the temple right away, perhaps by the redeemed who have returned with Him. It is not clear whether the Lord will allow this temple, built by unredeemed Israel, to remain through the Kingdom. What is clear is that a new Temple (the fifth) will be built during the Millennial Kingdom as we are informed of in Ezekiel chapters 40-43.

With Jesus in heaven (with the redeemed), it is best to see the opening of the first seal as the beginning of the Great Tribulation. And when we look at Revelation 6:9-11, "When He opened the fifth seal, I saw under the altar the souls of those who had been slain for the Word of God and for the testimony which they held. And they cried with a loud voice, saying, 'How long, O Lord, holy and true, until you judge and avenge our blood on those who dwell on the earth?' Then a white robe was given to each of them; and it was said to them that they should rest a little while longer, until both the number of their fellow servants and their brethren, who would be killed as they were, was completed'," several things can be noted. One is that the second, third and fourth seals are opened during the Great Tribulation. And this Great Tribulation is still going on during the time of the fifth seal. And as mentioned earlier, when we compare Matthew 24:29 and Revelation 6:12-13, it is best to view the Great Tribulation and the wrath of Almighty God as separate events. The opening of the seventh seal ushers in the Day of the Lord with the trumpet and bowl judgments. In Joel 2:31, this is called "the great and awesome Day of the Lord." And some of my favorite Words in Scripture follow, "And it shall come to pass that whoever calls on the Name of the Lord shall be saved..." You just have to call on His Name. I don't know how God could make it any easier and yet show His mighty power.

It is commonly accepted among some expositors of the Bible that the eighth chapter of Daniel refers to king Antiochus IV Epiphanes. And some see this prophecy as a dual reference to the anti-Christ. Without question, as Gabriel informed Daniel concerning his vision, it refers to the kingdoms of the Medes and Persians, that of Greece and the four kingdoms that arose after Alexander the Great died. Admittedly, not being an expert historian, but based on my studies, I can see how it could be taken as referring to either or both. It is clear that the visions of Daniel chapter seven as well as that of chapter nine, do refer to the anti-Christ. If one is to view this as a dual prophecy, then one, it seems, should take the whole account into consideration.

There are several hints that at the very least it should be seen as referring to both. In Daniel 8:9 we find, "And out of one of them came a little horn which grew exceedingly great toward the south, toward the east, and toward the Glorious Land." The beast certainly will rise to become exceedingly great as no other dictator in history. It seems that it is stretching the text to see Antiochus IV Epiphanes as exceedingly great or even very great as some translations have. In Daniel 8:23 the four kingdoms that arose from Alexander's kingdom, are viewed as one kingdom in latter time. God tells us, "And in the latter time of their kingdom, when the transgressors have reached their fullness (an indication of being very close to the "end" Jesus prophesied about), a king shall arise, having fierce features, who understands sinister schemes." This "latter time" seems to be referring to the same period as in Daniel 12:4, "But you, Daniel, shut up the words, and seal the book until the time of the end; many shall run to and fro, and knowledge shall increase." It was apparent to me we were in "the time of the end" and God confirmed it with me. I am not sure just when it began but I can speculate it started with the birth of the nation of Israel. The "end" probably refers to the end of the original covenant period when Christ will return to earth. In Daniel 8:24 we are told, "His power shall be mighty, but not by his own power." In Revelation 13:2 satan gives to the beast: "The dragon gave him his power, his throne, and great authority."

The most compelling reasons for me why the prophecy may refer only to the beast are found in Daniel 8:19 and 8:25. Gabriel told Daniel in verse 19, "And he said, 'look, I am making known to you what shall happen in the latter time of the indignation; for at the appointed time the end shall be'." This seems to point to the "time of the end" and the actual "end" itself. Then in Daniel 8:25 we see, "...He shall even rise against the Prince of Princes...", a clear reference to the One and only Jesus. Although Antiochus's vengeance against the Jews, desecrating their temple and later burning and killing many in Jerusalem, could be viewed as rising against the "Prince of princes", I would like to note something for consideration. At that point in history, the Word (Jesus) had not yet become flesh and according to John 1:1, "...and the Word was with God, and the Word was God." This direct reference to his "...rise against the Prince of princes", and the reference to the beast, along with the ten kings, will go against, amazingly, the One and only, the Almighty, as is my best guess Daniel chapter eight refers to the beast of Revelation. In Revelation 17:14 we see, "These will make war with the Lamb, and the Lamb will overcome them, for He is Lord of lords and King of kings; and those who are with Him, are called, chosen, and faithful."

Now I would like to discuss what has been called the revived Roman Empire. In Daniel 7:7, the prophet had a startling vision that included the fourth beast, "After this I saw in the night visions, and behold, a fourth beast, dreadful and terrible, exceedingly strong. It had huge iron teeth; it was devouring, breaking in pieces, and trampling the residue with its feet. It was different from all the beasts that were before it, and it had ten horns." This beast has been viewed, I believe correctly, as including the former Roman Empire which was noted for its use of iron. Also because the first three beasts have been identified as the Babylonian Empire, the Mede and Persian Empire, and the Grecian Empire respectively. The Roman Empire followed, becoming what was considered a world power at that time.

However, this prophecy is also seen as referring to a later power to come into existence that will be ruled by ten kings. We find in Revelation 17:10, "There are also seven kings. Five have fallen, one is, and the other has not yet come. And when he comes, he must continue a short time." This has been seen as the five kings of Rome, with one in John's time and the seventh unidentified. It is more likely the five that had fallen are: Egypt, Assyria, Babylon, Medo-Persia and Greece. And the sixth as Rome and the seventh as the one coming (with the ten kings) in the not too distant future. It is believed it will be in the area of the former Roman Empire. The fact that the beast is of the seven and is himself also the eighth is a good reason to see the first seven as kingdoms rather than all as individual kings. In Revelation 17:11 we are told, "The beast that was, and is not, is himself also the eighth, and is of the seven, and is going to perdition." Apparently he will become of the seven when he "...shall subdue three kings," as we are told in Daniel 7:24.

We are also informed of the Babylonian, Medo-Persian, Grecian and Roman kingdoms in Daniel chapter two. Daniel interpreted king Nebuchadnezzar's dream in verses 37-40, "You, O king, are a king of kings. For the God of heaven has given you a kingdom, power, strength, and glory; and wherever the children of men dwell, or the beasts of the field and the birds of the heaven, He has given them into your hand, and has made you ruler over them all-you are this head of gold. But after you shall arise another kingdom inferior to yours; then another, a third kingdom of bronze, which shall rule over all the earth. And the fourth kingdom shall be as strong as iron, inasmuch as iron breaks in pieces and shatters everything; and like iron that crushes, that kingdom will break in pieces and crush all the others." More details are in verses 41-43. To help us understand that the fourth kingdom would stretch to just before the Millennial Reign, God tells us in verse 44, "And in the days of these kings the God of heaven will set up a kingdom which shall never be destroyed; and the kingdom shall not be left to other people; it shall break in pieces and consume all these kingdoms, and it shall stand forever."

I would like to point out what we are taught in Scripture that will occur during the covenant time. Satan is the father of lies (John 8:44) and he is an imitator as well. In 2nd Corinthians 11:14 we see, "And no wonder! For satan himself transforms himself into an angel of light." There is God the Father, God the Son and God the Holy Spirit who are the Holy Trinity. And in Deuteronomy 6:4 we are told, "Hear, O Israel: The Lord our God, the Lord is one!" And lest anyone think that has now changed, we find in the Book of 1st John 5:7, "For there are three that bear witness in heaven: the Father, the Word, and the Holy Spirit; and these three are one." There is coming an unholy Trinity. Satan will choose a man to whom he will give his power, his throne, and authority" (Revelation 13:2). We see in Revelation 13:11-12, "Then I saw another beast coming up out of the earth, and he had two horns like a lamb and spoke like a dragon. And he exercises all the authority of the first beast in his presence, and causes the earth and those who dwell in it to worship the first beast, whose deadly wound was healed." These two beasts will not only have "the spirit who now works in the sons of disobedience" (Ephesians 2:2), but spirits of demons as we learn from Revelation 16:14. Satan himself will also have one. So we see satan trying to be like God the Father and the second beast acting like the Holy Spirit trying to get the world (and will succeed) to worship the first beast (who is to rule the world as Christ will, however vastly differently). The world will worship the dragon (satan) as well (Revelation 13:4).

Before I put everything in chronological order as I see it will happen, I would like to discuss something I believe has often been misunderstood. In 2nd Thessalonians 2:7 the Bible tells us, "For the mystery of lawlessness is already at work; only He who now restrains will do so until He is taken out of the way." Many, as I once did, believe "He who now restrains" refers to the Holy Spirit, and that the removal of the Church is planned here. Therefore it must occur before the signing of the seven year covenant. Now I do believe "the restrainer" is the Holy Spirit and He has restrained evil through the Church. However, even though Church attendance was much higher just before World War II began, that did not stop Hitler from bringing his (and satan's) evil on the world. My point is that God is able to remove Himself out of the way without leaving planet earth. I believe satan tried taking over the world during World War II and God restrained him through the Allies. Nevertheless, God will allow this, the taking over of the world, in the not too distant future. It is clear that even when the Church is removed, the Spirit of God will still be here. No person is saved apart from the work of the Holy Spirit, with God the Father beginning the process of salvation through Jesus. It is also clear that many will be saved during the Great Tribulation, according to Revelation 7:9-14, when the Church has been removed.

Though I will not include the following in the chronological order of events, I do wish to have you give it some consideration. In Ezekiel chapters 38-39, we are told about what is known as the battle of Gog and Magog. A large number of interpretations have been offered of these passages. In-Ezekiel 38:1 we see, "Now the word of the Lord came to me, saying, 'son of man, set your face against Gog, of the land of Magog, the prince of

Rosh, Meshech, and Tubal, and prophesy against him.'" Then in verse 5 we are told Persia, Ethiopia and Libya are included. In verse 6 also Gomer and all its troops and the house of Togarmah and all its troops. Though I don't think anyone aside from God knows the identity of them all, I think some have been correctly identified. I believe that Gog is indeed the leader and the land of Magog refers to Russia. Also that Iran, Libya, Turkey and Sudan are included in the coalition of forces. We learn in Ezekiel 38:16 what they will do, "You will come up against My people Israel like a cloud, to cover the land. It will be in the latter days that I will bring you against My land, so that the nations may know Me, when I am hallowed in you, O Gog, before their eyes." In Ezekiel 39:3-4 their outcome is assured by God, "Then I will knock the bow out of your left hand, and cause the arrows to fall out of your right hand. You shall fall upon the mountains of Israel, you and all your troops and the peoples who are with you; I will give you to birds of prey of every sort and to the beasts of the field to be devoured."

When considering the numerous times Russia has moved against Israel in the past, there is no reason to doubt they will do so once again, and this is in view in this prophecy. We can speculate that the energy crisis will be even worse in the not too distant future. Israel is known to contain large reserves of oil and gas. This coalition of forces will no doubt consist largely of muslims and as Israel's enemy would love to see her conquered. Israel is considered as a strategic land militarily as well. For these three reasons, it is easy to see or guess this may be why they think to go against Israel. We know that God is instrumental in bringing this about and may use this to ensure it.

In Luke 21:20 Jesus has told us, "But when you see Jerusalem surrounded by armies then know that its desolation is near." And in verse 21 Jesus said, "Then let those who are in Judea flee to the mountains, let those who are in the midst of her depart and let not those who are in the country enter her." While we are not told how long "near" is, verse 20 does correspond with Matthew 24:15, "Therefore when you see the abomination of desolation, spoken of by Daniel the prophet, standing in the holy place (whoever reads let him understand.)" And Luke 21:21 corresponds with Matthew 24:16-18, "then let those who are in Judea flee to the mountains. Let him who is on the housetop not go down to take anything out of his house. And let him who is in the field not go back to get his clothes." Now that is urgency!

I think that the armies that Jesus said would surround Jerusalem are none other than those of the Gog and Magog invasion. I believe God placed those verses before the others to give us a clue as to their identity. And it seems very possible that the invasion will occur really close to the midpoint of the covenant. While God has not confirmed that for me (and I have as yet to ask), it does seem to fit with the turbulent times unlike any others that will come just after, during the Great Tribulation. The desolation of Luke 21:20 Jesus spoke of is apparently the same one as when the antiChrist sets up his image (most likely) in the temple, in the area known as the Holy of Holies. The Holy of Holies, where the ark of the covenant was kept, was considered the most sacred part of the Tabernacle and Temple. After atoning for his sins, the High Priest, once a year, would enter to atone for the sins of Israel. He actually wore bells and as long as those outside kept hearing them, they knew God had accepted the sacrifice. God may supernaturally destroy these armies and cause some to believe in Him. It is clear that they will somehow be destroyed.

I have something else for your consideration which I will also not include in the chronological order of events a little later. As mentioned earlier, because it seems to overstate Antiochus IV Epiphanes reign in Daniel 8:9, that is, "exceedingly great" (or "very great" as some translations have), I think the little horn is none other than the antiChrist. If this is so, and I strongly suggest it is, then we can draw a conclusion about Daniel 8:13-14. The Bible states, "Then I heard a holy one speaking; and another holy one said to that certain one who was speaking, 'how long will the vision be, concerning the daily sacrifices and the transgression of desolation, the giving of both the sanctuary and the host to be trampled underfoot?' And he said to me, 'for two thousand three hundred days; then the sanctuary shall be cleansed.'" This allows two hundred and twenty days (give or take thirty days depending on your view of Daniel 12:11) for the Israelites to build their temple once the antiChrist confirms the covenant. It does not seem likely they will be safe to do so until then, even though they may be ready to build it beforehand. Daniel 8:14 tells us that their sacrificing (which will end in the midst of the covenant), and the temple which needs to be cleansed of the abomination of desolation

Jesus spoke about in Matthew 24:15, will involve twenty-three hundred days. It will cease at the end of the covenant period or shortly thereafter.

It is difficult not to think that the "falling away" of 2nd Thessalonians 2:3 has already come when the astonishing figures of Church attendance today are compared to seventy years ago. It is without a doubt in my mind that at least some of the Church will be able to recognize who the antiChrist is before we are gathered to Jesus. When one compares 2nd Thessalonians 2:7, mentioned earlier, with 2:8-9, we can easily see the logical order of events as I have explained they will occur. In verse 2:7 the restrainer, the Holy Spirit, is taken out of the way, probably by God the Father. Jesus has told us in John 10:29, "My Father, who has given them to Me, is greater than all; and no one is able to snatch them out of My Father's hand." In 2nd Thessalonians 2:8, the "lawlesss one is revealed". We are told, "And then the lawless one will be revealed, whom the Lord will consume with the breath of His mouth and destroy with the brightness of His coming." Verse 2:9 tells us, "The coming of the lawless one is according to the working of satan, with all power, signs, and lying wonders." So he is first revealed and then he is manifested. His manifestation will begin, it seems, with Jesus opening the first seal.

So now an overview of what will come prior to during the seventieth week of Daniel, at least in part. I can remember in the early eighties a large write-up in the newspaper in red (I no longer read the newspaper), about the European Economic Community (now called the European Union). There was speculation that this body was the ten kings and kingdom of Daniel 7:24. At present there are close to half a billion citizens in the European Union. And I believe it is likely that this is where the ten kings shall arise. At any rate, arise they will. This will be a kingdom but not a world-wide kingdom. The man who will become the beast will somehow subdue three of them, apparently peaceably and politically. He will then, or sometime afterward have enough clout to confirm the covenant with many. I suppose that from Daniel 7:24, "...another shall rise after them ... ", (referring to a king), placed before, "......And shall subdue three kings.....", could lead one to think he will confirm the covenant beforehand. While that seems possible, it is more probable that he will be able to guarantee their safety with more power. Again, the covenant will at least be with Israel, but the "many" may include, and seems likely to include, other countries in the region.

Prior to or not long after confirming the covenant (latter most likely), Israel will build its temple , the fourth one in history. The signer will enable them to reinstate their sacrificial system. I can only imagine the fervor among them at that time (I have heard they know how to throw a party!). For the first time in nearly two thousand years, they will be able to do as they were once commanded in the Old Testament. God did away with sacrifices by the one-time-for-all sacrifice in Jesus. Israel will shortly come to that conclusion as a nation.

There is no doubt that satanic persecution will be going on during the first half of the covenant, and I believe it will intensify, with it reaching a climax (but not near what is to come) around six months before the midpoint and lasting until the midpoint. As discussed earlier it seems that when accounting for the one thousand two hundred and ninety days of Daniel 12:11, one can conclude that it will begin thirty days from the midpoint. That is, the taking away of the daily sacrifice from Israel and the time of the abomination of desolation. Some have seen this abomination as the antiChrist himself, but I believe it will be the image of him that will be set up. In Revelation 13:14 we find, "And he deceives those who dwell on the earth by those signs which he was granted to do in the sight of the beast, telling those who dwell on the earth to make an image to the beast who was wounded by the sword and lived." Satan has deceived a great multitude throughout history to worship false idols who can't see, hear or talk. God will finally allow him to do something different. In Revelation 13:15 we are told of the false prophet, "He was granted power to give breath to the image of the beast that the image of the beast should both speak and cause as many as would not worship the image of the beast to be killed." This is enough to give some "the willies"!

As mentioned earlier it seems Jesus would desire to destroy the temple immediately after returning to earth. But knowing the patience of God, which is unlike any other, He may actually wait until a little while after He comes back. I can see how it can be viewed both ways with a good argument on each side. In Daniel 12:12, God tells us, "Blessed is he who waits, and comes to the one thousand three hundred and thirty-five days." This is forty-five days after the abomination no longer makes the temple desolate. In Ezekiel chapter 37 where we learn of the rebirth of Israel, we see in 37:14, "I will put My Spirit in you, and you shall live, and I will place you in your own land. Then you shall know that I, the Lord, have spoken it and performed it, says the Lord." In Matthew 24:31 we see just after the Lord's return, "And He will send His angels with a great sound of a trumpet, and they will gather together His elect from the four winds, from one end of heaven to the other." So there must be time to gather Israel, now saved as a nation, to their land. And then there must be time for Jesus to judge the nations. The "Blessed is he" of Daniel 12:13 are those who have survived the Great Tribulation, being in Christ, saved in their natural bodies. The rest will have to leave the earth. So all things considered, I think the twelve hundred and ninety days will stretch past the end of the covenant.

And so it seems easy to see the first half of the covenant as a more peaceable time (though it is a false peace), with the breaking of the covenant, the rapture and the war in heaven all occurring in a very short period of time. Then when satan and his angels are cast out of heaven (forever), he will persecute Israel. Israel is rescued from satan and taken into the wilderness. Then satan will go after Israel's offspring, what later are called the tribulation saints. This is the point when Jesus is opening the first seal, it seems, beginning the Great Tribulation. In fact what seems the scenario is that these three events will occur within a few days of the middle of the covenant: Then again, perhaps God will cause them to happen simultaneously. The Great Tribulation will last approximately three years and the wrath of God about six months. Toward the end of the covenant period, they will be gathered together to Armageddon. The kings of the earth and of the whole world will make war with the Lamb, as incredible as that is to me.

Now I shall give some details of some of what will occur either at the very end of the seven year period or very close to it, and some details afterward. In Revelation 19:11 we are told, "Now I saw heaven opened, and behold, a white horse. And He who sat on him was called Faithful and True, and in righteousness He judges and makes war." Both the holy angels and the holy saints will come to earth. Revelation 19:14 says, "And the armies in heaven, clothed in fine linen, white and clean, followed on white horses." These may be the saints only with Jesus. Though we know the angels go to earth, it is not clear from this passage if it will be at the same time (my best guess is yes). And in Zechariah 14:4 we are told, "And in that day His feet will stand on the Mount of Olives, which faces Jerusalem on the east. And the Mount of Olives shall be split in two, from east to west, making a very large valley; half of the mountain shall move toward the north and half of it toward the south."

In Revelation 19:20-21 we learn, "Then the beast was captured, and with him the false prophet who worked signs in his presence, by which he deceived those who received the mark of the beast and those who worshiped his image. These two were cast alive into the lake of fire burning with brimstone. And the rest were killed with the sword which proceeded from the mouth of Him who sat on the horse. And all the birds were filled with their flesh." It seems in the forty-five days of Daniel 12:12, Jesus will judge the nations, the unsaved will be killed and the saved in their natural bodies and those of us in our glorified bodies will enter the Millennial Kingdom. The saints who returned with Jesus will reign with Him! We see in Revelation 20:6, "Blessed and holy is he who has part in the first resurrection. Over such the second death has no power, but they shall be priests of God and of Christ, and shall reign with Him a thousand years."

Satan is bound for a thousand years in the bottomless pit so he is unable to deceive the nations as we see in Revelation 20:1-3. After the thousand years expires, he is released and deceives the nations, who are devoured by fire from God. Satan is cast into the lake of fire. These events are recorded in Revelation 20:7-10. What is known as the Great White Throne Judgment will apparently begin just after this as found in Revelation 20:11-15. And at some time called the "end", probably the end of the Millennial Kingdom, we learn from 1st Corinthians 15:24, "Then comes the end, when He delivers the kingdom to God the Father, when He puts an end to all rule and all authority and power."

In Revelation 21:1-2 we find great news! "Now I saw a new heaven and a new earth, for the first heaven and the first earth had passed away. Also there was no more sea. Then I, John, saw the holy city, New Jerusalem, coming down out of heaven from God, prepared as a bride adorned for her husband." Talk about a happy ending! Isaiah 9:7, I had God to tell me, teaches that this everlasting kingdom (see Daniel 4:3) will continually get better and better forever! "Of the increase of His government and peace there will be no end,... The zeal of the Lord of hosts will perform this." The gift we receive from God is truly indescribable! I would like to encourage you to read the Book of Revelation for more details. To God be the Glory!

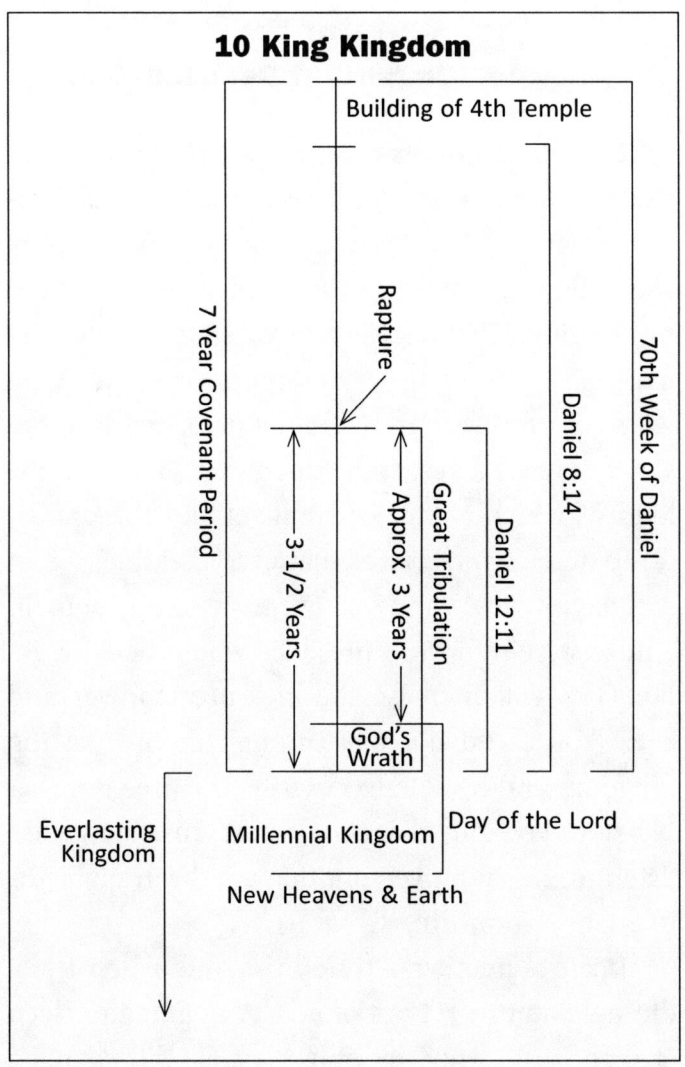

Chapter Six
Your Most Important Decision Ever

I have had doubts that I would be able to effectively express to you just how important this decision really is. However, having prayed fervently about it, I am trusting the Lord to guide me in my writing. This decision involves the wonderful truth of God giving us the opportunity of living with Him forever! To be free of pain, aggravation, sorrow, heartaches, harassment by satan, to the likes of which I am no stranger. And the opportunity to enjoy pleasures that exceed eating, sex in marriage (wow!) and yes even watching football! And just being in His presence would be enough, but God will increase the pleasures forever and ever! You could not talk through the everlasting kingdom and be able to describe this free gift that is before you this day (this to the unsaved-please listen to the audio version that will be available or to a Christ-honoring Church).

I can remember a time in my life when I just did not want to get out of bed. And going to sleep at night was really my only escape. God changed all of that...forever! Now I am not saying I do not have any problems, but I view them from a totally different perspective. Psalm 34:19 is still one of my favorite passages, "Many are the afflictions of the righteous, but the Lord delivers him out of them all." What a wonderful passage! God tells us ahead of time that troubles are coming but He will take care of and deliver us! In 2nd Timothy we are told, "Yes, and all who desire to live Godly in Christ Jesus will suffer persecution." Although all the righteous have problems, those of us who try to live Godly will have more. We will receive rewards for this. However God (being the perfect and more-than-perfect One that He is) has something for both groups.

Some people are satisfied with just being saved and not with rewards and live their life as a carnal Christian. These will not only incur loss of reward but will have to endure chastisement under the mighty hand of God (and from experience, it is grievous). And what does the God of gods do for our disobedience? Not punishment as some think but something only for our good. Hebrews 12:11 tells us, "Now no chastening seems to be joyful for the present, but painful; nevertheless, afterward it yields the peaceable fruit of righteousness to those who have been trained by it." Though some who desire to live in a Godly manner (as I did) backslide and need God to intervene as only He can. As we see in 1st Corinthians chapter 11, a Christian may sin to the point of death (as my dad did), but his/her soul will still be saved (see 1st Corinthians chapter 11).

For those of us who have set our hearts to live in a Godly manner, and for some of us who fail miserably at times, there is great news! The Book of Romans contains some powerful messages and wonderful truths. It captivates the hearts of theologians. It can be difficult to follow but with God's help it is possible to. Romans chapter 8 contains some of my favorite passages. Romans 8:18 says, "For I consider that the sufferings of this present time are not worthy to be compared with the glory which shall be revealed in us." God will reward those of us who willingly suffered for the cause of Christ.

Romans 8:28, "And we know that all things work together for good to those who love God, to those who are the called according to His purpose." This teaches us that whether it is pain, sorrow, sin (this is not an excuse to however), laughter or whatever, it all works for our good. The plain truth of the matter is that we just can't lose! Now I highly recommend for a new (or not so new) convert not to take the attitude that he/she can go out and do whatever they want and it will be ok. It just does not work that way (trust me on this), you will wish you had not! I have more than once wondered when satan is going to understand that while he has been giving us all of this trouble, in reality he has actually been helping us! While he has been incurring rewards in the negative, we, at least some of us, have been earning rewards in the positive. As God told me he still thinks he can win (and He actually referred to him as "dummy"), it will most likely be when he is put in the bottomless pit or later when he is cast into the lake of fire.

The Bible teaches that there are, in one respect, only two kinds of people with no middle ground. That is, those saved (in Christ) and those unsaved. Jesus said in Matthew 12:30, "He who is not with Me is against Me, and he who does not gather with Me scatters abroad." The Bible also teaches that Christians are in the kingdom of light and all others are in satan's kingdom of darkness. Christians are described in 1st Peter 2:9, "But you are a chosen generation, a royal priesthood, a holy nation. His own special people, that you may proclaim the praises of Him who called you out of darkness into His marvelous light."

Many people have wondered, and used as an excuse not to accept Him, how a Holy God would allow such evil to exist. I will be the first to admit I have been frustrated and puzzled at times with what God has done or allowed. In Romans 11:33 we are told, "Oh, the depth of the riches both of the wisdom and knowledge of God! How unsearchable are His judgments and His ways past finding out!" At times, knowing this, I have still tried to figure Him out to no avail. I have learned to accept His judgments and ways and understand He really does always know what to do, and His actions are always righteous.

In James 1:13 we learn more about God, "Let no one say when he is tempted, 'I am tempted by God'; for God cannot be tempted by evil, nor does He Himself tempt anyone.'" God never does evil but He certainly knows just how to use evil for good, as only He can. This has always been part of His Purpose. A good example of His doing this goes back before Christ walked the earth. Israel was in a state of rebellion and after God warned them through the prophets, He stirred up the Assyrians to defeat them and take them into captivity. It is commonly accepted that this occurred in seven hundred and twenty-two B.C. Here God used the evil of the Assyrians to chastise Israel to bring about good (as it did). He later punished Assyria for the evil they did. He treated Israel as a nation in a similar way as He does a child of His today. God is Sovereign in any and all situations both present, past and future. Because He is truly God of all, He can even use luck in His plan.

There have been volumes written on what one must do to be saved. Jesus told us in John 3:3 what we must do in order to go to heaven with Him, "...Most assuredly, I say to you, unless one is born again, he cannot see the kingdom of God." He spoke these words to the Pharisee Nicodemus concerning salvation and being able to enter the Millennial Kingdom. In the eighteenth century, the popular Reverend George Whitfield often preached on this subject of being born again. One day someone asked him why he spoke so much about it. I love what is really the only logical answer to that, He answered, "because you must be born again!"

Being born again involves inheriting a new nature. In 2nd Corinthians 5:17 we are told, "Therefore, if anyone is in Christ, he is a new creation; old things have passed away; behold, all things have become new." Many people believe that the world religions all point to the same God. Nothing is farther from the truth. If one will take the time to view them briefly, it is easy to see they all contradict one another and can't possibly all be right. And Jesus has plainly told us in John 14:6, "...I am the Way, the Truth, and the Life. No one comes to the Father except through Me." And then in Acts 4:12 we are told, "Nor is there salvation in any other, for there is no other name under heaven given among men by which we must be saved." That Name above all other names is Jesus!

In Romans 10:9-13 we are instructed on how to be saved, "that if you confess with your mouth the Lord Jesus and believe in your heart that God has raised Him from the dead, you will be saved. For with the heart one believes unto righteousness and with the mouth confession is made unto salvation. For the Scripture says, 'Whoever believes on Him will not be put to shame'. For there is no distinction between Jew and Greek, for the same Lord over all is rich to all who call upon Him. For 'whoever calls on the Name of the Lord shall be saved'." It is possible for one to have the intellectual knowledge of salvation without actually taking it to heart to be truly saved. I highly recommend if you believe yourself to be saved, that you examine yourself if you have not already done so. In 2nd Corinthians 13:5 we are admonished, "Examine yourselves as to whether you are in the faith. Test yourselves. Do you not know yourselves, that Jesus Christ is in you? -unless indeed you are disqualified."

Now, lest one of you out there thinks they have plenty of time to accept Christ as their Savior, I have a few things for you to consider. In 2nd Corinthians 6:2 we find one good reason not to delay one's decision, "...Behold, now is the accepted time; behold, now is the day of salvation." An unbeliever is not promised tomorrow. And Jesus makes this issue clear in Luke 13:4-5, "Or those eighteen on whom the tower in Siloam fell and killed them, do you think that they were worse sinners than all other men who dwelt in Jerusalem? I tell you, no: but unless you repent you will all likewise perish." To trust one's eternal destiny to a possible accident or other peril is most foolish indeed. And then in Matthew 24:48-51 Jesus has told us, "But if that evil servant says in his heart, 'My master is delaying his coming', and begins to beat his fellow servants, and to eat and drink with the drunkards, the master of that servant will come on a day when he is not looking for him and at an hour that he is not aware of, and will cut him in two and appoint him his portion with the hypocrites. There shall be weeping and gnashing of teeth.'" Sobering words indeed.

And now some other things for you to consider. In 2nd Thessalonians 2:9-12 we find, "The coming of the lawless one is according to the working of satan, with all power, signs, and lying wonders, and with all unrighteous deception among those who perish, because they did not receive the love of the truth, that they might be saved. And for this reason God will send them strong delusion, that they should believe the lie, that they all may be condemned who did not believe the truth but had pleasure in unrighteousness." This set of passages seem to teach that if you have had opportunity to accept Jesus as your Lord and Savior and do not, then it will be too late when that final time comes. The possibility of going into the Great Tribulation should be a strong enough reason to ask Jesus into your heart to save your soul. Many, many people will be killed during that time, saved and unsaved alike. Again, it will be a time unlike any other in history or ever will be. During the time of God's wrath, we are told in Revelation 9:6 it will be so bad that, "In those days men will seek death and will not find it; they will desire to die, and death will flee from them." I do not fully understand that but I believe it.

So give it up to the King and be blessed forever. The King of kings is coming, make no mistake about it, I am here to tell you. What I say to one, I say to all: "To God Be The Glory"!

Chapter Seven
To God Be The Glory

In this final chapter I would like to point out what I am sure of that Almighty God has revealed to me. I would also like to explain a great difference in the workings of God and satan. I have noticed even mature believers do not always get this right. In 1st Corinthians 14:33 we see, "For God is not the author of confusion but of peace, as in all the churches of the saints." Satan is no doubt creator of confusion. Many have believed that God confused the languages at the Tower of Babel. What he really did was confounded or mixed up the people by giving them different languages so that they could not continue their work as they wished. God has brought the Scriptures to us in a way we could only understand when the right time comes and only with His help. Meanwhile satan seeks to distort the Truth in as many ways as he possibly can.

It is without question that the original writings of the Holy Scriptures were without error. However, what has been brought down to us through the ages is in question by many. It is believed by experts in this field what we have is not entirely original. It is estimated we have ninety-five percent of the Old Testament and ninety-nine percent of the New Testament. While I am not an expert in this field, it would not surprise me if true. It would just tell me that God has allowed man to err. Even if this is true, there is some great news! God, the Holy Spirit, is the One who leads us into all Truth. Of that Truth I am certain and my trust is fully in God.

First, I was called as a prophet by God about fifteen years ago, though not realizing it. It was about two years ago that God told me to warn of the imminent return of Jesus. So with Deuteronomy 18:20 in mind, I tell you in the Name of Jesus the Christ that Jesus, the very Son of God and God Himself, the Almighty, is about to return to planet earth. I am certain He told me it was "at the steps", referring to the Church steps relative to the doors. And God confirmed the time line is close.

God also told me I would "teach like no other." I ask for your prayers concerning this and do not take this responsibility lightly. I have truly poured my heart into understanding the Scriptures through diligent study and asking God's guidance. And I will do so even more in the days ahead. I know this is God's will and count on Him leading us into the Truth as only He can. It is with great pleasure that I consider myself a friend of God and desire to serve Him faithfully in every area He so desires. I have only recently realized I have been called as an evangelist and I believe it will involve worldwide travel. God has confirmed to me that we are in "the time of the end" (see Daniel 12:4).

Although I believe we are in the apostasy period of 2nd Thessalonians 2:3, I see no reason God could not bring about a great revival. He did tell me that before He could bring a revival, that He Himself must be revived. I took this to refer to His zeal. Pray with me that He will bring about a third Great Awakening before Christ's return. I am not sure if this is in His plan but I hope so.

Please note that all the Scripture references in this book are from the New King James Version. This is because God told me to use it. Although He only told me specifically to warn of His return, there were other things confirmed to me. I hope these will in some way help the reader. He confirmed that there are literally seven Spirits of God (see Isaiah 11:2 and Revelation 1:4). These no doubt comprise the Holy Spirit, as the three persons of the Trinity are one God.

He also told me the elders of Revelation chapter 4 consist of, at the very least, part of the redeemed Church that is in heaven at that point. Probably some of the Old Testament saints as well. This is in the first half of the covenant and confirmed as such. Though I am sure it will be toward the end of that period, the timing is speculation but I think it is correct. Revealing the timing (approximate) of the rapture, enabled me to speculate that events of Revelation chapter 6 will begin the Great Tribulation. The events of chapters 4-6 could occur in a very short period of time and though not confirmed, I believe it is correct.

The last thing I can remember God confirmed for me at the time of this writing (though more may come back later), is a truly wonderful Truth which seems to be a perfect ending for this book. The "increase" of Isaiah 9:7 refers, even though without would be great, to things getting better and better throughout the everlasting kingdom. That is difficult to fathom but I believe it. God is so good that He is willing to give those who were once wretched sinners, His best in Jesus and then bless us more and more forever! Though I believe the gift of Christ is itself indescribable, no wonder we can't describe all the gift involves because it just continually increases! If you have any doubt about this, consider the size and beauty of the second heaven where the stars are located. As we are told in Psalm 19:1, "The heavens declare the glory of God; and the firmament shows His handiwork." If you take the time to research its size as far as we know it, it is enough to boggle the mind. I love it! So again, what I say to one, I say to all: "To God Be The Glory"!

Printed in the United States
141159LV00001B/1/P